A Place in the Sun

FAVOURITE DESTINATIONS

A Place in the Sun

FAVOURITE DESTINATIONS:
A guide to buying your dream home in
Spain, Italy, Portugal and France

Introduction by Amanda Lamb

Fanny Blake

First published 2002 by Channel Four Books, an imprint of Pan Macmillan Ltd,
Pan Macmillan, 20 New Wharf Road, London N1 9RR
Basingstoke and Oxford
Associated companies throughout the world
www.panmacmillan.com

ISBN 0 7522 6506 7

A CIP catalogue record for this book is available from
the British Library.

Design by Perfect Bound Ltd
Maps created by ML Design
Colour reproduction by Aylesbury Studios Ltd
Printed and bound in Great Britain by Butler and Tanner,
Frome and London

This book accompanies the television series *A Place in the Sun*
made by Freeform Productions for Channel 4.
Executive producers: Ann Lavelle and Antoine Palmer
Series Producer: Stephanie Weatherill

Notes

The prices given for properties visited by house-hunters are
accurate for the exchange rate at the time of the visit.
The author, their assigns, licensees and printers cannot accept
liability for any errors or omissions contained herein nor
liability for any loss to any person acting as a result of the
information contained in this book. This book gives advice on
the basis that readers contemplating buying a property abroad
take their own professional advice.

Picture credits

5 (from top) The Travel Library/Stuart Black, The Travel Library/Philip
Enticknap, The Travel Library/R. Richardon, The Travel Library/John
Lawrence; 7 Freeform Productions; 8 The Travel Library/Stuart Black;
12 The Travel Library/Sam Howard; 14 Turespaña; 15 The Travel
Library/Stuart Black; 16 The Travel Library/Stuart Black; 17 The Travel
Library/Lee Frost; 18 The Travel Library/Philip Enticknap; 19 The Travel
Library/Stuart Black; 20 The Travel Library/Ch. Hermes; 22 The Travel
Library/ Philip Enticknap; 23 The Travel Library/Ch. Hermes; 24 (top) The
Travel Library/Roger Howard (bottom) The Travel Library/Philip
Enticknap; 26 Travel Ink/Ronald Badkin; 28 The Travel Library/Stuart
Black; 30 Freeform Productions; 31 Channel 4 Television; 32 (top) Channel
4 Television (rest) Freeform Productions; 33 (top) Freeform Productions
(bottom) Channel 4 Television; 34 Channel 4 Television; 35 Channel 4
Television; 36 Lesley Handford and Bob Foad; 37 Channel 4 Television;
38 (top and below left) Channel 4 Television (below right) Lesley
Handford and Bob Foad; 39 (top) Freeform Productions (below) Channel
4 Television; 40 Channel 4 Television; 41 Channel 4 Television; 42 John
and Fiona Simm; 43 John and Fiona Simm; 44 Pat and Jan Beasley; 45 Pat
and Jan Beasley; 46 Tony and Christine Martin; 47 Tony and Christine
Martin; 48 The Travel Library/Philip Enticknap; 52 The Travel
Library/Stuart Black; 54 The Travel Library/Philip Enticknap; 57 The Travel
Library/Philip Enticknap; 58 The Travel Library/Richard Glover; 60 The
Travel Library/Stuart Black; 61 The Travel Library/John Lawrence; 62 The
Travel Library/Philip Enticknap; 63 The Travel Library/Ch. Hermes; 65 The
Travel Library/Philip Enticknap; 66 Travel Ink/Ronald Badkin; 68 Channel
4 Television; 69 Channel 4 Television; 70 Channel 4 Television; 71 Channel
4 Television; 72 (top left) Susanne and Justin Finden-Crofts (top right and
below) Channel 4 Television; 73 Channel 4 Television; 74 Matthew Smith
for Sonia Coady and Graham Ditchfield; 75 Matthew Smith for Sonia
Coady and Graham Ditchfield; 76 Wanda and Graham Nash; 77 Wanda
and Graham Nash; 78 Travel Ink/R. Richardson; 82 The Travel Library/Ch.
Hermes; 83 Portuguese Tourism Office; 84 The Travel Library/David
Robertson; 85 The Travel Library/H. G. Schmidt; 86 Travel Ink/Chris North;
87 Portuguese Tourism Office; 88 Travel Ink/Simon Reddy; 89 Travel
Ink/Abbie Enock; 90 Travel Ink/Abbie Enock; 91 (left) Portuguese Tourism
Office (right) The Travel Library/R. Richardson; 92 (top) The Travel
Library/Stuart Black; 92 (bottom) Portuguese Tourism Office; 93 Travel
Ink/Ronald Badkin; 94 The Travel Library/Stuart Black; 95 The Travel
Library/Roger Howard; 97 (top) The Travel Library/Stuart Black;
97 (bottom) Portuguese Tourism Office; 98 Channel 4 Television;
99 (top) Channel 4 Television (bottom) Richard Whiteley and Kathryn
Apanowicz; 100 Richard Whiteley and Kathryn Apanowicz; 101 Channel 4
Television; 102 Channel 4 Television; 103 Channel 4 Television; 104 Bob
Hughes; 105 Portuguese Tourism Office; 106 José and Edwin Boothby;
107 José and Edwin Boothby; 108 The Travel Library/John Lawrence;
112 The Travel Library/Stuart Black; 113 The Travel Library/Stuart Black;
114 The Travel Library/Stuart Black; 116 Travel Ink/David Martyn Hughes;
117 The Travel Library/John Lawrence; 119 The Travel Library; 120 The Travel
Library/Stuart Black; 122 Travel Ink/David Martyn Hughes; 123 The Travel
Library/Philip Enticknap; 125 The Travel Library/Roger Howard; 128 The
Travel Library; 130 (top) Freeform Productions (bottom) Channel 4
Television; 131 Channel 4 Television; 132 Paul Bennett and Deena Harris;
133 Channel 4 Television; 134 Channel 4 Television; 135 (top) Channel 4
Television (bottom) Lesley Cooper and Stuart Robinson; 136 (top)
Freeform Productions (bottom) Channel 4 Television; 137 (top) Channel 4
Television (bottom) Freeform Productions; 138 (top) Channel 4 Television
(bottom) Emma and Geoff Sallows; 139 Channel 4 Television;
140 Channel 4 Television; 141 Channel 4 Television; 142 Robert and Susan
Kirk; 143 Robert and Susan Kirk; 144 Peter Dawson and Marilyn
Seabrooke; 145 Peter Dawson and Marilyn Seabrooke; 146 Sandy and
Emma Swinton; 147 Sandy and Emma Swinton;148 Bob Camping;
149 Travel Ink/Ian Booth

Thanks

The author and publishers would like to offer particular thanks to Bob
Hughes of West Coast Real Estate, Vivian Bridge of North & West France
Properties Ltd, Linda Travella of Casa Travella, and Sarah Gear,
researcher, for their help. Thanks also to John Howell & Co for
assistance with legal sections.

Contents

Introduction

by Amanda Lamb

Welcome to *A Place In The Sun: Favourite Destinations*. It seems like only yesterday that I was writing the introduction to last year's book, but here we are, twelve months on, with a whole new series of shows and a brand-new cast of househunters looking to take the plunge and find their dream homes abroad.

For those of you unfamiliar with the programme, *A Place In The Sun* aims to help prospective buyers of properties in Europe and beyond, by acting as a sort of cross between an estate agent and a tour guide. We find the househunters a selection of properties which fit their aesthetic, geographic and budgetary requirements, offer practical advice, put them in touch with local experts, give them a tour of the region, pointing out the downsides as well as the attractions of the area, and then sit back and see what happens. Of course, it is immensely satisfying when we find our househunters their dream home, but sometimes their appearance on the show is only the first step on what can be a long, complicated ladder to buying a property abroad.

During the course of the past three years, we have travelled all over the world in our quest to match househunters with their own place in the sun. However, for this book, we are going to focus on the countries that attract the most attention from Britons wanting to buy property abroad: France, Spain, Portugal and Italy. The popularity of these four European destinations remains undiminished. They are the places we are, perhaps, most familiar with, having holidayed there. They are geographically close to Britain, making the logistics of looking for and buying a property a little more manageable than in countries on the other side of the world. Their cultures are relatively accessible for us, and European employment legislation means that we can, if we wish, assimilate further by working there. But perhaps the biggest draw of all is the climate, and the attendant values and attitudes to life that seem to accompany blue skies and abundant sunshine. How many of us dream of whiling away a lazy afternoon sipping cappuccino in a trattoria, watching the world go by? Or wandering around whitewashed, sleepy mountain villages, the air redolent with citrus and pine? Or strolling along a deserted beach at sunset? For most of us, these are brief holiday snapshots. For many of our househunters, they become the daily grind! No wonder *A Place In The Sun* is attracting an ever-growing army of viewers.

In this book, we look at the benefits and potential pitfalls of buying property in these four countries, and feature a selection of typical and unusual dwellings. We also look at the practical side of living in France, Spain, Portugal and Italy, with a general guide that will answer at least some of your questions. And, my favourite bit, we meet up with househunters from the earlier series, and find out how they have fared since relocating. Fascinating and inspiring stuff.

Finally, before you dive into the book and start making your own plans to sell up and head for the sun, a note of caution. This is only meant to be a general guide to buying property and living abroad, it is definitely not a substitute for the professional advice that

any prospective buyer should seek at home and in the host country. Any additional costs incurred by employing a lawyer or financial advisor could save you from making an extremely expensive mistake. Even if that achingly beautiful bougainvillea-draped farmhouse has your name written all over it, it might not, after closer inspection, have the vendor's name on the deeds! Always try to let your head rule your heart. That said, there are some truly fantastic properties out there just waiting to be discovered, and one of them really could be yours, a place in the sun to call your very own. Bonne chance!

Amanda Lamb, June 2002

Spain

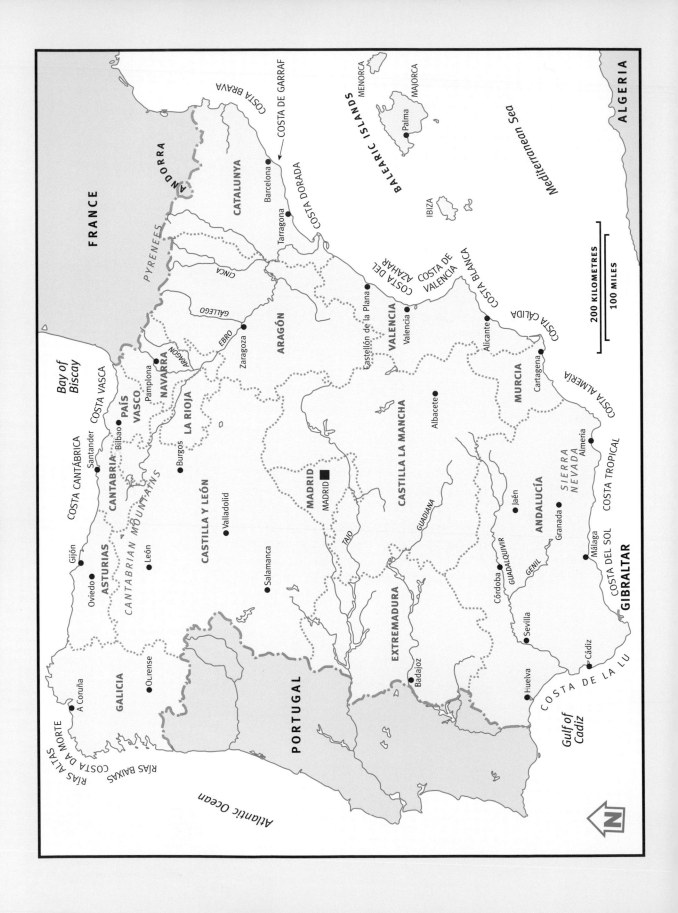

Spain

Spain is a land of excitement. It is blessed with blazing sunshine, clear seas, dramatic landscapes, beautiful wines and fierce brandies. The stamp of the flamenco dancer, the thrum of guitars, the roar of the crowds at football, bullfight, nightclub or fiesta, all add a tang of urgency and passion to the atmosphere. Yet for many of the 700,000 Britons who have bought property there, Spain possesses other qualities in addition to these: a life less stressful and more healthy, with the added benefits of a warmer, drier climate, a sounder diet, and good healthcare and education systems. Inland, away from the tourist hot spots, Spain still preserves the time-honoured notions of hospitality, honour and respect.

Long ago, the Iberian peninsula was prized by foreign invaders, among them the Phoenicians, Romans and Visigoths. During the eighth century, large parts of it fell to the Moors, an Islamic people who crossed from North Africa, and it was not for another six centuries that a united Spanish nation (and eventually the hub of a vast, overseas empire) emerged. Even then, the people strongly adhered to their regional identities, most notably the Basques and the Catalans who even retained separate languages.

The Bourbon dynasty was established by the War of the Spanish Succession (1701 1714) but its increasingly ineffectual rule was violently interrupted in the twentieth century by a leftist revolt and a Civil War, followed by the long years of General Franco's repressive, backward-looking dictatorship. Since Franco's death in 1975, and under the more liberal and very popular figurehead of King Juan Carlos, Spain has joined the European Union and made huge strides in democracy and development. Many rural areas have become depopulated as a result of the migration of labour to the towns, which has left some villages virtually empty. But, at the same time, the quality of Spanish life overall has been on the upward path, with major advances in healthcare, social services, communications and education. Throughout this varied history, however, one thing which has remained constant has been the Spanish character, with its unrivalled sense of drama, and its simultaneous devotion to the relaxed spirit of *mañana* – enjoy today and defer what you cannot enjoy until tomorrow.

regions

Spain may be best known for the magnificent beaches and pulsating resorts of 'the Costas'. However, look inland and the geographical diversity is vast. Andalucía offers spectacular, mountainous sierras, Almería boasts a parched, Arizona-like landscape and the windy plain of La Mancha is renowned for its windmills, legendarily tilted at by Don Quixote. In the north-west lies lush, green Galicia, geographically isolated and offering a remarkable contrast to the arid central tableland or *meseta central*. In the north-east is Catalonia, one of Spain's great cultural and industrial regions.

Madrid, the capital, is at the geographical centre of the country and is the seat of the central government. The second major city is Barcelona, capital of Catalonia and

facts

CAPITAL: Madrid
AREA: 504,782 sq km
COASTLINE: 4,964 km
POPULATION: 40,050,000
CURRENCY: Euro
TIME ZONE: GMT + 1 hour
ELECTRICITY: 220 volts
WEIGHTS AND MEASURES: metric
RELIGION: Roman Catholic
LANGUAGE: Castillian (Catalan, Galician, Basque)
GOVERNMENT: parliamentary monarchy
INTERNATIONAL DIALLING CODE: 00 34
INDEPENDENCE: 1492
NATIONAL HOLIDAY: Hispanic Day, 12 October

deemed by many to be by far the most lively and interesting. There are other cities of great charm and tradition too, however, such as Seville, Córdoba and San Sebastián.

Since 1975, devolution has left Spain with 17 autonomous regions, each of which has its own parliament and government, jealously guarding its ancient individual character and customs. Each region is also justly proud of its food and wines which depend on the climatic variations throughout the country.

Andalucía

LANDSCAPE: white, sandy beaches with rugged cliffs along the coast, spectacular mountainous scenery inland, particularly the Ronda and Sierra Nevada

PROVINCES/MAJOR TOWNS: Almería, Córdoba, Granada, Málaga, Seville, Huelva, Jaén

COASTLINE: Costa de la Luz, Costa del Sol, Costa Tropical, Costa de Almería

HIGHLIGHTS: flamenco dancing, bullfights, Ronda (gorge and old Roman aqueduct), white villages, Parque Natural de Cazorla, las Alpujarras, Sierra de Grazalema

FESTIVALS: *Semana Santa* (Seville, Easter), *Feria de Abril* (Seville, April), *Romería del Rocío* (Seville, May or June), *Carnaval* (Cádiz, February), horse fair (Jerez de Frontera, May)

HANDICRAFTS: pottery, leatherwork, woodwork, glassware, hand-woven rugs

FOOD: *pescado frito* (fried fish, Seville), *salmorejo* (soup with eggs and ham), *rabo de toro* (bull's tail), *ajo blanco* (almond and garlic soup), Serrano ham, *pescaíto froti* (mixed fried fish), *urta al la roteña* (fish stew)

DRINK: Cruzcampo beer, sherry

AIRPORTS: Jerez, Málaga, Seville

Aragón

LANDSCAPE: ranges from the Pyrenees and breathtakingly beautiful national parks in the north through dry areas down to the mountains in the south-east

PROVINCES/MAJOR TOWNS: Huesca, Teruel, Zaragoza

HIGHLIGHTS: Parc Nacional y Monte Pedro, Parc Nacional de Ordesa, *mudéjar* architecture (Teruel, Zaragoza), Castillo de Lorre

FESTIVALS: *Las Tamboradas* (Teruel province, Easter), *Carnaval* (Huesca, February/March),

Romería de Santa Orosia (Huesca, June), *Día del Pilar* (Zaragoza, October)

HANDICRAFTS: blue and white pottery (Muel), green and purple ceramics (Teruel)

FOOD: *migas de pastor* (ham with breadcrumbs), *chilindrón* (stew of lamb, poultry and peppers), *melocotónes* (wine-soaked peaches), *frutas de Aragón* (fruit dipped in chocolate)

DRINK: red wines from Cariñena, Campo de Borja; white wines from Somontano

AIRPORT: Zaragoza

Asturias

LANDSCAPE: mountains, heavily wooded areas and a rocky, rugged coastline

MAJOR TOWNS: Oviedo, Gijón

COASTLINE: Costa Verde

HIGHLIGHTS: Picos de Europa, Llanes, pre-Romanesque architecture

FESTIVALS: Festival of *San Mateo* (Oviedo, September), *Fiesta del Pastor* (Vega del Enol, July), Cider Festival (Gijon, August), *Semana Grande* (Gijón, August)

HANDICRAFTS: black pottery, clogs, lace, leatherwork, penknives (Tarramundi)

FOOD: *fabada asturiana* (stew), *repollo relleno*

de carne (stuffed cabbage), *merluz a la sidra* (hake in cider), *arroz con leche* (rice pudding)
DRINK: cider
AIRPORT: Oviedo

Cantabria

LANDSCAPE: mountainous inland, with white, sandy beaches and rugged cliffs along the coast
MAJOR TOWNS: Santander, Torrelavega, Reinosa
COASTLINE: Costa Cantábrica
HIGHLIGHTS: beaches, palaeolithic cave paintings (Altamira), Parc Natural de Oyambre, Santillana del Mar
FESTIVALS: *Semana Grande* (Santander, July), *Festival Internacional de Santander* (August), *La Folia* (San Vicente, April), Battle of the Flowers (Laredo, August)
FOOD: *cocido montanés* (bean stew), *marmita* (bean, tuna and potato stew), *raba* (squid), *campurriano* (chicken and rice)
DRINK: Sierra Cantábrica (red rioja); brandy from Orujo
AIRPORT: Santander

The scenic landscape of inland Andalucía attracts many British home buyers seeking an escape from it all.

Castilla La Mancha

LANDSCAPE: prairie land used for cereal crops and dotted with windmills
MAJOR TOWNS: Albacete, Ciudad Real, Cuenca, Guadalajara, Toledo
HIGHLIGHTS: *Casas colgadas* (Cuenca), Toledo, windmills, Tablas de Daimiel
FESTIVALS: *La Endiablada* (Cuenca, February), *Romería del Cristo del Sahúco* (Albacete, May/June), Feast of Corpus Christi (Toledo, ninth week after Easter), Feast of the Assumption (Toledo, August)
HANDICRAFTS: metalwork, ceramics, lace, embroidery, Damascene weapons, knife-making
FOOD: *gazpacho manchego* (meat stew), *migas* (breadcrumbs and garlic), *queso manchego* (cheese), wheat soup, *pisto manchego* (tomato stew), *perdiz estofada* (stuffed partridge), game dishes, marzipan
DRINK: red wines from Valdepeñas
AIRPORT: Madrid

Castilla y León

LANDSCAPE: vast plains stretching to hills capped with castles

PROVINCES/MAJOR TOWNS: Ávila, Burgos, León, Palencia, Salamanca, Segovia, Soria, Valladolid
HIGHLIGHTS: cathedrals at Burgos and Léon, Alcazár, Roman aqueduct (Segóvia), Ávila, University of Salamanca (Burgos), monastery (Santo Domingo de Silos)
FESTIVALS: Festival of San Juan and San Pedro (Segovia, June), Festival of Santa Teresa (Ávila, October), St Agatha's Day (Zamarramala, February), fire-walking (San Pedro Manrique, June), *El Colacho* (Castrillo de Murcia, May/June), International Trout Festival (León, June), festivals to celebrate the bull farms in the region (Salamanca, September)
HANDICRAFTS: blankets, gold jewellery
FOOD: *cochinillo asado* (roast piglet), *sopa castellana* (egg and garlic soup), *queso de Burgos* (cheese with honey), *morcilla* (blood, rice and tripe sausage)
DRINK: red wines from Ribera del Duero and Toro; rosés from Rueda; black wines from Cigales
AIRPORT: Valladolid

Catalonia

LANDSCAPE: from the dramatic, snow-covered Pyrenees to orange-grove filled valleys and sandy beaches with rugged cliffs
COASTLINE: Costa Brava, Costa Tropical, Costa Daurada, Costa del Garraf
PROVINCES/MAJOR TOWNS: Barcelona, Girona, Tarragona, Lerida
HIGHLIGHTS: Roman ruins (Tarragona), Teatre-Museu Dali (Figueres), Parc Nacional d'Aigüestortes, La Sagrada Familia Cathedral (Barcelona), monastery of Montserrat, Romanesque buildings
FESTIVALS: *Fiesta de Tarragona* (July/August), wine festival (Figueres, September), La Patum (Berga, Corpus Christi ninth week after Easter), human castles at many festivals, food festival (Lerida, May), Dance of Death (Verges, Easter), Midsummer's Eve (everywhere)
HANDICRAFTS: yellow and green pottery, glassware
FOOD: *pa amb tomaquet* (bread covered in garlic, tomatoes and oil), *botifarra dolca* (sweet pork sausage), *zarzuela* (mixed seafood), *arròs a la Catalana* (paella)
DRINK: red wines from Priorato, whites and cava from Penédes
AIRPORTS: Barcelona, Gerona

Extremadura

LANDSCAPE: remote, wooded sierras, with mountains and valleys in the north

PROVINCES/MAJOR TOWNS: Badajoz, Cáceres

HIGHLIGHTS: Roman remains (Mérida), Monfragüe Natural Park, monasteries of Guadalupe and Yuste, Templar towns in the south, Trujillo

FESTIVALS: *Férias de Cáceres* (May/June), *Ferias and Fiestas de Trujillo* (June), *Semana Santa* (Guadalupe, September/October), *Féria* (Mérida, September), *Carantoñas* (Acehuche, January)

HANDICRAFTS: lace, honey, copperware, gold jewellery

FOOD: *perdiz al estilo* (partridge), *caldereta* (lamb or goat stew), *chanfaina* (offal stew), *ancas de rana* (frog's legs)

DRINK: white wines – Cañamero and Chiclana

Galicia

LANDSCAPE: fertile, hilly interior with an occasionally rocky coastline sliced by *rías* (fjords)

PROVINCES/MAJOR TOWNS: A Coruña, Pontevedra, Lugo, Ourense

COASTLINE: Rías Baixas, Costa da Muerte, Rías Altas

HIGHLIGHTS: Santiago de Compostela, Pontevedra, pilgrimage walk to Santiago de Compostela from French border

FESTIVALS: *Día de Santiago* (Santiago de Compostela, July), *Romería Vikinga* (Pontevedra, August), *A Rapa das Besta* (Pontevedra, May/June), *Os Peliqueiros* (Laza, February/March)

HANDICRAFTS: porcelain, earthenware, lace

FOOD: *caldo gallego* (vegetable soup), *pulpo a gallego* (octopus), *churrasco* (grilled meat/ribs), *pimientos de Padrón* (green peppers with garlic), *tarta de Santiago* (almond cake)

DRINK: white wines – Albariño, Turbio Condado; red and white Ribeiros; beer – Estrella de Galicia

AIRPORTS: Santiago de Compostela, Vigo

Comunidad de Madrid

LANDSCAPE: capital city on central plateau, with sierras in the north

MAJOR TOWN: Madrid

HIGHLIGHTS: Palacio Real, Museo de Prado (art gallery), the Parc del Retiro, old Madrid, El Escorial, Alcalá de Henares, Chinchón, Palacio Real de Aranjuez

FESTIVALS: *Cabalgata de los Reyes* (Madrid, January), *Carnaval* (Madrid, February), *Fiestas de San Isidro* (Madrid, May)

FOOD: *tapas* (originated here), *cocido madrileño* (meat stew), *callos* (stewed tripe), *soldaditos de pavía* (salted cod)

AIRPORT: Madrid

Murcia

LANDSCAPE: fertile coastal plain with citrus groves, vineyards and market gardens, becomes mountainous and arid further inland

MAJOR TOWNS: Murcia, Cartagena

COASTLINE: Costa Cálida

HIGHLIGHTS: Parc Natural de Sierra España, Catedral de Santa María (Murcia), Santuario de la Vera Cruz (Caravaca de la Cruz)

HANDICRAFTS: crib figures

FESTIVALS: *Semana Santa* (Lorca, Easter), Race of the Wine-Bearing Horses (Caravaca, May), *Bando de la Huerta* (Murcia, Easter)

FOOD: *torta Murcia* (chicken/sausage frittata), sweet pepper salads, baked fish, snails

DRINK: red wines from Jumilla; reds, whites and rosés from Yecla

In Cantabria, the village of Santillana del Mar has kept many of its traditional dwellings intact.

The façades of fishermen's houses in Valencia's Vilajoyosa were painted such vivid colours so that their owners could identify them from the sea.

País Vasco

LANDSCAPE: mountainous, green interior with rugged coastline
PROVINCES: Guipúzcoa, Álava, Vizcaya
MAJOR TOWNS: Bilbao, San Sebastián, Vitoria-Gastiez
COASTLINE: Costa Vasca
HIGHLIGHTS: Guggenheim Museum (Bilbao), Bilbao old town, *El Bosque Pintado de Oma*, traditional sports, e.g. pelota
FESTIVALS: *Festival de Jazz* (Getxo, Vitoria, San Sebastián, July), *Festividad de San Sebastián* (January), *Aste Nagusia* (Bilbao, August), *Fiesta de la Virgen Blanca* (Vitoria, August)
HANDICRAFTS: Damascene weapons, gourds and wine containers
FOOD: *bacalao a la vizcaína* (cod), *chipirones en su tinta* (young squid along with their ink), *pintxos* (regional tapas), *baba-txikis* (bean soup), *kokotxas* (hake fritters)
DRINK: Txakoli (white wine), cider
AIRPORTS: San Sebastián, Bilbao

Rioja

LANDSCAPE: green pastures and vineyards stretching from the foot of the Sierra mountain range
MAJOR TOWN: Logroño
HIGHLIGHTS: dinosaur footprints (Enciso), Santo Domingo de la Calzada Cathedral, Monasterio de Santa María la Real (Nájera)
FESTIVALS: *Fiesta de San Mateo* (Logroño, September), *Fiestas de la Vendimia* (Logroño, September), *Fiesta de San Bernabé* (Logroño, June), Wine Battle (Haro, June), ancestral stilts dance (Anguiano, July/September)
HANDICRAFTS: woven blankets and carpets
FOOD: *patatas a la riojana* (potatoes with peppers), quail with beans, *sopa de ajo* (garlic soup)
DRINK: Rioja wines (red, white and rosé)

Navarra

LANDSCAPE: mountainous, green scenery of the Pyrenees, with cultivated plains and sierras in the south
MAJOR TOWNS: Pamplona, Tudela
HIGHLIGHTS: Lumbier gorge, Tudela cathedral, Monasterio de Leyre, Valle de Roncal
FESTIVALS: *Sanfermines* (bull running, Pamplona, July, Estella, July/August)
HANDICRAFTS: leather gourds and wine containers
FOOD: *bacalao al ajoarrieri* (salt cod with garlic), *aldereta ribereña* (stew), *perdiz a la tudelana* (partridge with apples), *cordero en chilindrón* (lamb, garlic and peppers)
DRINK: wines – Chivite (red), Gran Feudo (rosé)

Valencia

LANDSCAPE: busy coastline with palm, olive, citrus and almond groves inland, rising to sierras
PROVINCES/MAJOR TOWNS: Alicante, Castellón, Valencia
COASTLINE: Costa Blanca, Costa de Azahar
HIGHLIGHTS: Valencia Cathedral, Morella, Elche and surrounding palm forest, Roman ruins (Sagunto), *Els Ports* (mountain passes),

Museo Popular de Arte Contemporáneo (Vilafamés)

Festivals: *Las Fallas* (Valencia, March), Moors and Christians (Alcoy, April), *Festiu de Juliol* (Valencia, July), Festival de Saint Joan (Alicante, June), *Festa Major* (Denia, July), *Fiesta de la Tomatina* (Buñol, August)

Handicrafts: ceramics, lustreware, leather goods

Food: *paella* (originated here), *arroz a banda* (fish with rice), *all i pebre* (fried eels), *sepia con salsa verdi* (cuttlefish)

Drink: white and rosé wines from Utiel-Requena; Agua de Valencia (champagne and orange juice).

Airports: Valencia, Alicante

Balearic Islands
(Ibiza, Mallorca, Menorca, Formentera)

Landscape: Ibiza – beautiful beaches on the coast, and mountains inland; Mallorca – rocky and white sand beaches, olive groves; Menorca – hilly in the north, flatter in the south

Major towns: Eivissa (Ibiza), Palma (Mallorca), Mahón (Menorca)

Highlights: beaches, Catedral de Palma, nightlife (Ibiza), Castillo del Belver

Festivals: *Día de San Juan* (Mallorca, June), *La Fiesta de San Juan*, (Menorca, July)

Handicrafts: pottery, ceramics, majolica, rushwork and basketry, woollen goods

Food: *sopas mallorquinas* (vegetable soups), *cnsaimada*s (cakes), *huevos a la sollerica* (eggs and sausage with a pea sauce), *berenjenas rellenas* (stuffed aubergines), *tumbet* (peppers, potato and tomato), *ensaimada* (spiral-shaped bun)

Drink: white and rosé wines from Binissalem and Majorca; liqueurs (including herb and almond); gin from Menorca

Airports: Ibiza, Mallorca, Menorca

The brilliant white houses at Menorca's Binibeca Vell provide comfortable holiday homes.

Property

By far the majority of foreigners looking for a place in the Spanish sun head for the coast. Despite the spectacular amount of development over the last forty years, there still seems to be enough sun, sand and space to go around. The most popular areas tend to be those in close proximity to an airport, the most popular of all being the Costa del Sol: 160 km of sun-baked coastline crowded with residential and tourist development. Demand for property is as high as ever, with prices tending to increase approximately 20 per cent each year. The most expensive area is the Golden Mile running from Málaga to Marbella, with its neighbouring area stretching from San Pedro to Estepona, named the 'New Golden Mile' as it takes up the overflow. Developments west of Estepona command lower prices but are considered good investments as roads are being improved and building work completed. Similarly, east of Málaga is becoming more popular and urbanizations are springing up in what until now has been a more rural landscape, with some attractive small towns offering original town houses. Developers are driven by demand, and own vast stretches of land along the coast, which makes it virtually impossible for an individual to find land and obtain planning permission. If drawn to a more tranquil, rural way of life where your money will go further, head inland to the Andalucian *pueblos blancos* (white villages). Whitewashed to deflect the sun's heat, houses of varying sizes are joined together in narrow streets. Their narrow frontages can disguise surprisingly large interiors. Small windows keep the heat out and are sometimes decorated with wrought-iron grilles. Some houses have flat roofs which can be used as living space in the summer, and some have gently sloping roofs with terracotta tiles. Many of them are built Moorish-style, around a courtyard. In the countryside, there are *latifundios* (large houses with land) and *cortijos* (farmhouses), but these are becoming increasingly hard to come by now, as many foreign buyers have moved inland, having already realized that they can have the luxuries of space and privacy only a short drive from the coast.

Outside the Andalucian town of Granada lies a countryside of golden summer fields.

The Costa Blanca, from Denia to the Mar Menor, is another hot spot, with about 50 per cent of its foreign home owners stemming from the UK. The capital, Alicante, and the major resorts of Jávea and Denia command the highest prices, which have risen between 25 and 30 per cent in the last three years. There are plenty of resorts north of Alicante, with ever-increasing development in the south, especially around Torrevieja. Inland, the landscape changes dramatically, giving way to sleepy villages built of local stone (predominantly limestone and rubble), and houses with wooden beams. Most of the houses have been added to as the families have grown, leaving very few with gardens or patios. *Casitas del campo* are usually built from breezeblocks and often have land attached, making them popular with British buyers. However, it is

important to check that the building is not registered as an agricultural construction but as a house, as otherwise planning permission may be hard to come by. Property is in demand in this area and in some places prices have doubled between 2000 and 2002. The Costas Cálida and Almería around the Mar Menor are still thought of as a relatively undiscovered part of the Spanish coastline, although the Spanish have been holidaying there for years. Again, thanks to the low-cost airlines and the opening of a new coastal motorway, the area has opened up to British buyers. As a result, the prices are on the up but as yet it is still one of the cheaper coastal regions of Spain. Perhaps the most expensive part is the exclusive La Manga resort area, where prices have risen 20 per cent in the last year alone. Inland, naturally, money goes further when buying a renovated *finca* or a village house with distinctive Spanish characteristics and opting for a quieter, more relaxed way of life.

Among the up and coming areas where you will get more property for your pound are the Costa Brava, Costa de Azahar, Costa de la Luz and Galicia, with its recent boom in rural tourism. The north-eastern Costa Brava, from the border to Barcelona, has less reliable weather than the south, but is growing in popularity with British buyers. It is particularly popular with non-flyers because of its accessibility by road through France. Towns popular with the British include Begur, Estarret, Pals, Palamós, and, most expensively, Aiguablava, where prices have been rising steadily due to increased demand. Few ex-pats buy inland, beyond the motorway running between Gerona and Barcelona, but even on the coast side this does not restrict them to urbanizations. Old villas and farmhouses can still be found for restoration, although they can be expensive, while more modern '60s villas are also popular buys.

Further south, lies the Costa de Azahar (Orange Blossom Coast) between Barcelona and Valencia. Buying here, property owners get a taste of real Spain in the picturesque fishing villages. Only a twelve-hour train journey from London, and with a new airport

Whitewashed houses in steep, narrow streets lead from Cadaqués' Iglesia de Santa Maria down to the natural harbour.

in construction, the area is rapidly gaining in popularity, with some prices doubling in the last few years, but more generally rising by 20 to 25 per cent. Available properties range from apartments to semi-detached and detached villas. Traditional properties are large and offer great value for money, if you can persuade a Spaniard to part with one. It is also possible to buy land and obtain planning permission, although the town halls are becoming stricter about imposing limitations. There are only a few completed complexes, and while construction work continues, prices remain among the lowest on the Costas. Traditional properties outside the inland villages tend to be large *fincas*, which are great value for money but only rarely come onto the market.

With tourism still to gain a foothold, the Costa de la Luz still remains virtually undiscovered by the British home buyer. On the south Atlantic coast, from Tarifa to the Ayamonte, it offers kilometres of unspoilt beaches, without any high-rise buildings, and with vigilant environmentalist groups aiming to make sure it stays that way. The major complex developments are around Huelva, whose main attraction is its golf courses, but a lesson has been learned from its neighbour, the Costa del Sol, and building work is being very carefully controlled. Within the long stretch of pine forest bordering the beach there are low, discreet urbanizations. The land here is particularly valuable, so prices are on the up. There are old properties, apartments, town houses and *cortijos*. The architecture is typically Andalucían: white-washed houses with roof terraces and tiles both in and out, with a hint of Portugal creeping in on the decorative chimneys seen near the border. Land near the coast is hard for the individual to find, thanks to developers snapping it up, but further inland, small plots are available.

Another largely undiscovered treasure is the province of Galicia. What it lacks in sunshine, it makes up for in its lush landscape and unscathed coastline. Prices are much lower than on the Mediterranean coast but rising steadily. The west and south-west coasts tend to attract more foreigners simply because they are a little sunnier. The choice of property is between urbanizations and large, traditional, stone farmhouses (*pazos*), which typically have three or four bedrooms as well as outbuildings. Of these, the *horreo* (a granary on stilts) is regarded as a prize, and must be kept intact. The houses themselves are typical of the northern regions of Spain. They have steeper pitched roofs to protect against the weather, overhanging caves for shelter and often wooden balconies on the first floor. Originally, animals were kept on the ground floor, the living quarters were in the middle, and upstairs was used for storing produce.

The Balearic Islands of Majorca, Menorca and Ibiza have offered attractive bolt holes for many foreigners seeking an escape from it all, with the result that prices are higher than on the mainland. Building restrictions are tighter than they have ever been and property is at a premium. The coastlines tend to offer apartments or villas in new resorts and

Almería's Velez Blanco is dominated by its impressive sixteenth-century castle.

traditional town houses in the major towns and villages; while inland you will generally find *casas payesas* (cottages), which are usually single-storey buildings with all of the rooms leading off a main one. Walls are thick, roofs flat and windows small or non-existent, and frequently there is a covered area outside.

The primary property market in Spain is in new or relatively new property along the coast, close to beaches or one of the many golf clubs. The Spanish have realized that throwing up crowded, sky-high developments will simply ruin their coastline, and so developments are now restricted and building standards higher. Not everywhere is as developed, so a choice exists between moving into a strictly British enclave abroad and moving somewhere less subject to the whim of the tourist season. Some urbanizations are predominantly British, while others have a high proportion of Spanish and other foreign residents, some permanent. There are also a few complexes that cater exclusively for retirees, providing various care facilities. By far the majority of foreigners buy holiday homes in a complex or urbanization. These vary enormously, depending on the number and type of properties and the range of facilities on offer. They may include apartments, semi-detached or attached town houses, or individual villas, which may be new or resale properties, or may be bought off-plan, i.e. at the planning stage. Buying off-plan can be a sound investment, since the value inevitably rises as the surrounding environment is completed. Each property must come with a ten-year structural guarantee. When looking at a show house, make sure you understand exactly which features are included in the price you have been quoted. You may be able to choose your own bathroom and kitchen fittings, carpets, tiles and so on. You may even be able to alter the layout of the internal space to suit your needs better. Buying off-plan involves a slightly different process from buying a finished property. Usually, payment is made in agreed stages as the building work proceeds. It is vital that you, or your appointed representative, check that the work has reached the required standard at each stage. It would be wise to check that the infrastructure of the community is complete before buying – or you may find yourself fighting for the construction of roads, shops or a pool that you believed you had paid for.

Buying property in an *urbanización*, which shares facilities between owners, means automatically becoming a member of the *Comunidad de Propietários* (Community of Property Owners). This is the Spanish system for regulating the joint ownership of common property. It is run according to the majority vote of the owners, while ensuring the rights of the minority are protected. A *presidente* (chairman) is elected every year to represent the owners and make sure affairs are conducted properly. Every member pays an annual fee that is set by the *Comunidad* and has the right to attend the annual general meeting (AGM). The *Comunidad* ensures the upkeep of such things as gardens, pools, installations and buildings, security and facilities, deciding how much to spend on them and how they should be managed. Before buying a property, it is worth checking a number of things. Find out how much the annual charges are and what they cover. Ask for a copy of the statutes so that you can see what regulations are enforced. Ask the vendor for a certificate showing that his community fees are paid, otherwise you may be liable to pay up to a two-year backlog. Ask for the minutes of previous AGMs to see whether there have been any problems, what developments are being planned and whether you will be expected to pay extra contributions. Check whether the Community is in debt and whether you might be called on to pay extra to bring it back into the black. Finding answers to all these

The ancient walled quarter of Ibiza Town winds beneath the cathedral and enjoys a splendid view of the city and harbour below.

questions will save you trouble and money in the future.

If buying an old property to restore, there are a number of important considerations to make before taking the plunge. First of all, be realistic about the amount of time and work it will take to bring it up to scratch. If you are not going to be living in Spain while the work is happening, you will need to find a reliable architect and project manager (possibly the same person) to oversee the building work. Also, be aware that although you may long for an idyllic mountain retreat, when it comes to reselling, it may be difficult to find a buyer easily. Might that matter? Before buying, it is vital that you or your solicitor check the ownership thoroughly. Thanks to Spanish inheritance law, older properties are often owned by numerous members of a family, all of whom must agree to the sale. Tracking them down may hold up the sale or even prevent it from going through. Some old properties may not have deeds, in which case ownership has to be documented by the local court. When buying in a village, it is wise to check out the local water supplies. Has there been a history of water cuts? If buying in a more remote area, it is common for the houses not to have running water, sanitation or electricity. It is essential to find out whether mains services can be connected to the property and the cost of doing so. If the property has its own well, check the water supply. Your proposed site may be in a spectacular situation off the beaten track, but make sure that you have the right to access it across the fields from the road – the landowner may be difficult. When considering a ruin, check the deeds to see that it is registered as a dwelling and not as an agricultural construction. It may be problematic getting it re-registered. Similarly, if a plot of land is not registered in the Land Registry, getting it registered may be difficult. If building from scratch, rebuilding, adding an extension, or altering the external doors or windows, planning and building permission will have to be obtained from the local town hall. Make sure a conditional clause is included in the contract (see below) to release you from the purchase if the permissions are not forthcoming. If buying a plot of land, be aware that there will be a *derecho de retracto*, which means the adjoining landowner with the smallest amount of land should be given the opportunity to match your offer, but only if he is going to use it to increase the size of his agricultural property.

If the proposed property needs modernizing, it is wise to bring in a surveyor (*arquitecto técnico*) to check it over. Alternatively, an architect or builder may do this for you. Whenever possible, employ people through personal recommendation and, especially in the case of an architect, look at some of his or her previous work. Before signing a contract, get an estimate of the costs of the work proposed so that there will not be too many nasty shocks in store. Note that when the work has been completed, a *declaración de obra nueva* (declaration of new work) should be made, otherwise the capital gains tax may be extortionate when it comes to resale.

Whatever property you decide to buy in Spain, don't let the sun go to your head and do not be pressurized by enthusiastic estate agents. Take your time to do all the necessary homework, so that you can be assured that what you buy will indeed be your dream place in the sun.

how to find a property in Spain

Spanish property exhibitions take place all over the UK throughout the year (advertised in property magazines and local papers). They are an ideal way of seeing the kinds of property available and a good starting point for finding out the sort of information that may be useful. Inspection flights are frequently on offer. If you decide to take advantage of the offer, don't let yourself be pressurized by the company concerned into buying anything you are not 100 per cent positive about. Having decided on the area in which you want to live, look on the Net, where you will find numerous estate agents and details of their properties. The English and Spanish national newspapers are another source of information, as are specialist magazines such as *Spanish Homes*, *World of Property*, *Homes Overseas* or *Spain*. There are a

A typical cobbled street in the medieval village of Pais, Catalonia.

number of publications in Spain for ex-pats, such as *The Entertainer*, the *Weekly Post*, *Costa Blanca News* and *Sur*, which, among other things, advertise property, and all of which have their own websites.

When choosing a Spanish estate agent, make sure they are professionally qualified and registered with a professional association such as GIPE (*Gestor Intermediario en Promociones de Edificiones*). Check whether or not they are professionally indemnified. There are plenty of estate agents operating who are not licensed and who may be unscrupulous and too keen on getting their sale. Remember that the estate agent is not there to make the necessary checks on your behalf. Strictly speaking, an estate agent can manage the entire purchasing process in Spain without the need of a solicitor. However, they may not be expert in investigating the legal information regarding a property, so it is a wise safeguard to appoint a solicitor. Estate agents' fees vary and can be between 5 and 15 per cent, usually to be paid by the seller. If you buy through a British agent operating with Spanish sub-agents, the fee should be split between them, meaning that it should not cost you any more than if you were solely using a Spanish agent. If you are unable to find the professional help you need through personal recommendation, a good estate agent should be able to recommend someone to you, and may also be able to arrange such things as mains connections and even the rental of your holiday home when you are not using it.

How to buy a property in Spain

What follows is a general guide. There is no substitute for professional advice on individual circumstances. It is recommended that you have contracts professionally checked before signing them. It is also important to decide in whose name the deed should be registered because of inheritance implications (see below).

Each sale varies in its detail. You may want to employ the services of a specialist English solicitor, a Spanish lawyer or a *gestor*, a licensed professional who, for a reasonable fee, will act as the middleman between you and the Spanish bureaucracy. A *gestor* is not a solicitor, but can handle your paperwork for the purchase of a property, your application for residence, your taxes, setting up a business and more. Your *gestor* or your solicitor will conduct searches to ensure various aspects of the purchase are going as planned: checking that you are buying what you think you are buying in terms of the property and surrounding land; checking that the seller has legal title to the property; checking that there are no unpaid debts accrued against the property; ascertaining whether there are any building restrictions imposed by the local authority, and so on.

Traditional Majorquin houses enjoy a tranquil setting overlooking the Mediterranean.

Generally, when you have chosen your property, a private contract (*contrato privado de compraventa*) is drawn up, which specifies details of the buyer and seller, the purchase price, a deposit (usually 10 per cent), the completion date, the method of payment, any extras you have agreed to buy and any other relevant terms or conditions. This is a binding contract and your deposit can only be refunded under certain strict conditions. Make sure you understand what these are. It is common practice for the sale and purchase price to be understated so that the seller's liability for capital gains tax is reduced. Remember, when you come to sell and the actual price is declared, you will be liable to pay tax on the additional profit.

If you are buying 'off-plan', i.e. the property is still being built, payments will be made in agreed stages that vary according to the developer. You, or your representative, must check the work is completed satisfactorily at each stage. Make sure that the contract allows you to get a bank guarantee covering you against the risk of the seller going bust before finishing the project. The law requires the seller to give it.

The purchase is usually completed up to three or four months later in front of the notary (*notario*), whereupon the final deed (*escritura de compraventa*) is signed by you or someone you have invested with power of

attorney. Property is sold in the condition it is in at the time of completion, so it should be checked by you and/or your representative. At this point, the balance of the money is due and the keys will be handed over. After signing, your lawyer will pay the taxes due and lodge the deed with the Land Registry to register the change in title formally. This may take three months or more, by which time Land Registry fees are due. The *gestor* should give you a copy of the deed, so that your lawyer can complete the other legal formalities. The registration is vital. Even after you have signed the contract, charges can be registered against the property without your knowledge until it has been registered in your name. The notary's fees are set by the government and are due after completion. You should budget approximately 10 per cent of the purchase price to cover the additional taxes, land registry fees, notary fees and legal fees.

mortgages

If you choose to take out a mortgage in Spain with a Spanish lender, do not expect the process to be identical to the British. It is up to the bank how much they will lend. There is no fixed maximum. Factors such as income, profession, marital status and employment status may all be taken into account. Some banks will lend up to 80 per cent without proof of income, but this usually only occurs in the case of new developments. Spanish mortgages are among the most competitive in Europe and are most commonly of the variable interest type. The bank will register a first charge on the property with the land registry. You are not legally obliged to take out a home insurance policy with your mortgage provider, although they may strongly encourage you to do so. As always, it is much better to shop around until you find the lender that suits you best.

The mortgage granted will be a percentage of the official value of the property, i.e. lower than the market value. You can expect to be granted up to 80 per cent for a primary residence or between 50 and 60 per cent for a holiday home. The repayment term is most commonly between ten and fifteen years.

When budgeting for your purchase, remember to include the fees attached to setting up the mortgage. They can be significant. If borrowing in Euros, remember that exchange rate movements may increase the cost of repayments. If any problems with repayment do arise, it is sensible to contact the lender immediately and negotiate a rescheduling of payments. Repossession of Spanish property can and does happen with the additional possibility of forfeiting your money. Financial penalties incurred for late payment can be severely punitive. There may be UK tax implications, so take professional taxation advice to ensure that the documentation complies with both UK and Spanish law.

insurance

Taking out third-party liability insurance is optional. When taking out adequate household insurance to cover damage and theft, watch out for small print which may invalidate any claim if you are out of the country for a certain period of time. If your property is part of a complex, check exactly what is covered by the community insurance. Make sure third-party liability is included.

inheritance law

Spanish inheritance law dictates that the children of a deceased have an inalienable right to fixed portions of a property, but a foreigner resident in Spain can dispose of his property according to the law of his home country. It is crucial to make a Spanish will disposing of your property in the way you wish. But first, seek professional legal advice. The Spanish authorities may well acknowledge a will made in the UK, but it will take considerable time to process it and tax penalties may be incurred if not dealt with speedily. A Spanish will makes inheritance and succession much simpler for those you leave behind. There are three types of will, the most common of which is a *testamento abierto* (open will), prepared by a notary and signed in front of three witnesses. The notary retains the original copy, gives a copy to you and registers one with the *Registro Central de Ultima Voluntad*. Otherwise you might choose a *testamento cerrado* (closed will) whose contents are kept secret. Prepared by a lawyer it is given to the notary in a sealed envelope for him and the witnesses to sign. Alternatively, you can draw up a *testamento ológrafico* (holographic will) in your own handwriting, but authentication of such a will after your death could prove troublesome.

Opposite: New villas in Cala Tirant, Menorca, have been built in traditional Moorish style.
Below: The Parque Natural de los Picos de Europa is an area of outstanding natural beauty in northern Spain.

Living in Spain

residency

EU residents may enter Spain for up to 90 days before applying for a temporary residency card. A permanent residency card lasts for up to five years. An application form from the *oficina de extranjeros* or *comisaria de policía* must be accompanied with proof of sufficient means of support (income, employment contract, bank balance) and health insurance. If you do not wish to apply in person, a *gestor* will handle it for you.

fiscal representative

Non-residents owning a property must appoint a fiscal representative. This must be someone, whether a friend, lawyer or tax adviser, who lives in Spain and who will be prepared to receive mail from the tax authorities and to pay any taxes or bills on your behalf. Although not a legal requirement for a non-resident owning a single property, appointing a fiscal representative is a step that may remove a few headaches.

NIE (Número de Identificación de Extranjeros)

This is an identification number needed by all residents and non-residents with second homes. It is obtained from the Foreigners' Department of the local police station.

work

EU nationals do not need a work permit to work in another member country. However, it will be hard to find professional employment without a working knowledge of the language.

social security

Spain operates a social security system (*Seguridad Social*) that is similar to the one used in the UK and covers most of the population for a full range of welfare provision. If you

government

Spain is a constitutional monarchy with a Head of State (king or queen). There is a bicameral *Cortés Generales* (Parliament), composed of the *Congreso de los Diputados* (Chamber of Deputies), and the *Senado* (Senate), both elected through universal suffrage. The country is divided into seventeen *Comunidades Autonómicas* (autonomous communities/regions), each funded by the central government and with its own parliament, president, government, administration and Supreme Court (plus its own flag and capital city). The regions of the Basque Country, Catalonia, Galicia and Andalucía have been granted more autonomy than the rest. The regions are divided into fifty provinces. Each province has its own administration which is responsible for a range of services, including health, public works, sports facilities and social clubs. The provinces are subdivided into *municipios* (municipalities), town and district administrative units. The *municipios* are run by a council elected with other council members every four years and headed by an *alcaide* (mayor). The council offices are in the *ayuntamiento* (town hall), where each councillor is responsible for a different area of local services.

pets

There are no quarantine procedures, but you will have to provide an international health certificate signed by a vet registered with the Ministry of Agriculture. This needs to be issued no more than two weeks before departure. If you want to take your pet back into the UK, you will need to get a pet passport.

continue to pay your NI contributions in the UK you will be entitled to a UK pension. However, if you are working in Spain, this won't be necessary because your contributions to the Spanish system will count towards your UK pension. Consult leaflet SA29 (from the DSS) for details of social security, pension rights and healthcare within the EU.

furniture and goods

An EU citizen establishing a permanent residence in Spain can transport any furniture and goods into Spain free of customs duties, provided he/she has owned them for more than six months.

Andalucía is renowned for its white villages where houses are frequently adorned with wrought-iron balconies and grilles.

pensions

If retiring to Spain, it is a wise precaution to take some pension-planning advice. Pensioners are entitled to receive their UK state pension, receiving the annual increases and Christmas bonus. If you are a Spanish resident, then you must declare any private pension as part of your worldwide assets and pay Spanish tax on it. If you have already paid UK tax on it, you can claim to have it refunded or set off against the Spanish tax owed.

bank account

Would-be residents are wise to open a Spanish bank account before they move, thus simplifying the procedure of paying for professional advice and any bills. The procedure is much the same as in the UK. Alternatively, for non-residents, it is a simple matter to apply through one of the larger UK banks with Spanish branches or through a UK branch of a major Spanish bank.

taxes

INCOME TAX – RESIDENTS: You are deemed a resident of Spain if you spend more than 183 days of the calendar year in the country. There are other considerations qualifying residency, so it is a wise precaution to take professional advice regarding your individual situation. Residents are taxed on their worldwide income and assets. Non-residents are taxed only on the money earned from their activities in Spain and on the basis of their assets located in Spain. It is each individual's responsibility to get a tax form from the *gestoría* and to submit it with the appropriate payment. The tax year runs with the calendar year. Non-payment or late payment is met with fines or penalties.

INCOME TAX – NON-RESIDENTS: A non-resident must make an annual tax return, detailing any income received in Spain, including rental income and any interest accrued on Spanish bank accounts. If the property is not let, you will be expected to pay a small tax based on the notional letting value of the property. This is a fixed percentage of the *valor cadastral* (official value). The income will also be declared in the UK but the double taxation treaty between Spain and the UK means tax must only be paid once. Returns must be filed between 1 May and 20 June.

CAPITAL GAINS TAX: Capital gains are not taxed separately in Spain, but as part of a resident's taxable income. When it comes to property, the prices used to calculate the tax liability are those on the title deed. So, if the original purchase price was under-declared you may be liable to a large capital gain when declaring the actual resale price. In the case of sales by non-residents, capital gains tax is 35 per cent. A capital gain must be registered within three months. If buying property from a non-resident, the buyer must deduct 5 per cent of the purchase price and pay it with a completed form 211 to the Ministry of Finance. This acts as a guarantee that the vendor will pay his CGT. Otherwise, the buyer may be liable.

WEALTH TAX: The *Impuesto Extraordinario Sobre el Patrimonio* is a small tax levied on residents and non-residents. It shows the value of all an individual's assets located in Spain. This should be paid in June each year.

INHERITANCE TAX: Spain imposes an inheritance tax if a deceased owned property or assets in Spain. The tax must be paid by the beneficiaries within six months of the death if it occurred in Spain. The amount payable depends on the beneficiary's relationship to the deceased, the amount inherited and the beneficiary's current wealth. It is important to take legal advice on this and any possible avoidance tactics when deciding under whose name to register a property when buying it.

VAT: The standard rate is 16 per cent.

local taxes

IMPUESTO DE BIENES IMMUEBLES (IBI) is payable annually. Based on the official value of the property, it varies according to its size and location. Each municipality sets their own rate depending on the services it provides and the area. Make sure the official value (commonly about 70 per cent of the market value) has been correctly assessed before buying the property. Also check that all back taxes have been paid.

PLUS VALIA is a small tax based on the increase in value of the land since the last sale. It is officially paid by the vendor, although usually it is passed on to the buyer, depending on your private contract.

TASAS Y CARGAS are small charges raised by municipalities to cover the costs of local services such as rubbish collection or street cleaning.

education

The Spanish education system has undergone considerable changes over the last decade, bringing it into line with other European systems, although it still maintains something of its reputation for a traditional and disciplined approach to learning. This has great appeal to many British parents. Education is now compulsory between the ages of six and fifteen, with the majority of four- and five-year-olds voluntarily attending state or private nurseries. In the state system, parents are usually expected to buy books, and also to contribute to school supplies, transport arrangements or extra-curricular activities. At the end of primary schooling, pupils receive either the *Título de Graduado Escolar* entitling them to secondary education, or the *Certificado de Escolaridad*, qualifying them for technical training courses. Compulsory secondary education now lasts for four years and leads to the *Graduado en Educación Secundaria*. The final two non-compulsory years of secondary schooling take two forms. A student successfully completing the *Bachillerato*, an academic preparation for university, will be awarded the *Título de Bachillerato*. To enter university, they have to sit an exam (*Selectividad*). Alternatively, a student may take two years of technical training (*Formación Profesional*) to receive the *Técnico Especialista* certificate. The Spanish university system has its roots in the Middle Ages, with the foundation of the University of Salamanca in 1218. The end of the twentieth century saw the greatest growth in the university system as it moved towards decentralization and self-government. Classes can be huge (2000 people attending a lecture) and the study is much less personalised than it is in the UK.

Parents with young children may feel that entering them into this system (whether state or private) is a sure way of immersing them in their new society. To enrol a child in a school, you will need to arrange an interview at the school, having applied to your local authority in the UK to convalidate the schooling your child has received so far. He or she may be admitted on a temporary basis while waiting for the convalidation. You will also need proof of residence, along with your child's passport and certificates of immunization. Those with older children may prefer to consider

cars

A foreign car can be imported providing it has been registered in the owner's name for over six months. After compulsory re-registration in Spain, it cannot be sold within the first year. All vehicles must have an annual check (ITV) after the first four years. Non-residents can drive on a foreign licence for six months. EU residents can use their existing licence until it expires, but must then apply for a Spanish licence.

schooling them in one of the many international schools that exist in many of the major towns. They may also feel more confident that these schools will offer familiar syllabuses that will be more readily recognized in their home country should they return. There are schools offering French, German, American and UK education systems, some combining them with Spanish teaching or Spanish studies giving the student the possibility of living and working in either Spain or the UK.

healthcare

The Spanish national health system INSALUD (Instituto de la Salud) offers free (or low-cost) medical and dental treatment to any resident paying social security contributions or receiving a retirement pension. If you have paid National Insurance contributions in the UK for more than two years, you are entitled to treatment under the scheme for a limited time. You will need an E106 from the DSS. Pensioners will need to produce an E121 to receive equivalent benefits in Spain. Members of INSALUD receive a *cartilla* (social security card) which they need to show when receiving treatment. You will be given the name of a local doctor or clinic, but it is possible to change doctors within the area, provided there is room for you on their list. If you are in any doubt as what you are entitled to, check with the DSS before you go.

The unforgettable sight of Ronda, perched above the Guadalevín ravine.

However, although the quality of healthcare is usually good in Spain, the waiting lists for specialists and non-urgent operations can be long, and in outlying districts the health services can be inadequate. This makes it advisable to take out private medical insurance as well. If you are ineligible for public health benefits, it is essential. Proof of insurance will be necessary in order to obtain a residence card. Shop around to find a policy that suits you, making sure you read all the small print, checking what is and is not covered, particularly if you are approaching retirement.

Non-residents should have an E111 (from their local post office in the UK) entitling them to free emergency treatment while in Spain as a tourist. Normally, you will pay the doctor and then reclaim the fees as directed on the E111 form. Taking out extra insurance cover is also recommended.

mains services

ELECTRICITY: Electricity is supplied by a number of companies, the principal ones being Groups Endesa, Iberdrola, Union Fenosa and Hydroeléctrica de Cantábrico. Immediately after buying a property, you should sign a contract with the local company, showing a copy of your contract, usually your passport or residence card, plus the previous owner's contract and bills. You may need to pay a deposit and, if a non-resident, give details of your foreign address or fiscal representative. In a community property, connection fees are included in the selling price.

GAS: Mains gas is only available in the major cities in Spain. Again, contact the local company when moving into a property to have it connected. The gas will be metered and you will be billed every two months. Alternatively, many people use gas bottles for cooking and heating. The bottles can be replaced by a butane gas replacement service that operates in most areas.

WATER: The mains water supply is controlled by the local municipalities or may be the responsibility of a private company. Apply to whichever is appropriate for connection or for the installation of a water meter. There is usually a quarterly charge for a minimum consumption and bills are sent every two months.

House hunters

Costa de Garraf
Ben and Amita Butler

The Costa de Garraf is a nineteen-mile stretch of coastline just south of Barcelona. Named after the mountain range that rises behind it, it enjoys some of the best weather in northern Spain with hot summers and mild winters. The small fishing villages, once strung along the coast, have given way to some of Catalonia's more cosmopolitan resorts. Only half an hour from Barcelona and close to the airport, it is popular with both local commuters and foreign home buyers, with the result that property there is highly sought after, a fact that is reflected in the prices.

Ben and Amita Butler had both worked in films and commercials but since the birth of their daughter, Jaya, Amita had become a full-time mother, while Ben continued to work as a cameraman. They had decided to move to Spain permanently, having holidayed there for nine years, believing it to be a much healthier environment in which to bring up Jaya. Their priorities were the house itself but also the location because Ben was going to continue working in England, so needed to be close to an airport, while Jaya needed to be close to a school. 'We'd love to have something traditionally Spanish, but we do want space, and a pool would be nice.'

SITGES is a cosmopolitan resort town. It started life as a fishing village, but then came to prominence during the 1890s as a centre for the avant-garde art world. It has a rich cultural diary, with theatres and cinemas, jazz festivals and an annual Carnival. Evidence of the Moorish occupation is still present in the architecture, but the town buzzes with life, with plenty of contemporary shops and restaurants, and seventeen beaches, two of which are nudist. It attracts every kind of holidaymaker and has a large, international gay community, as well. Its demand is such that property prices are among the highest in Spain.

Above: Ben and Amita Butler changed their lives by moving to Spain for good. Below: A villa just outside Sitges offered spectacular views and opportunities for a comfortable, modern lifestyle.

Just outside the town was an unfinished, four-bedroom, modernist villa perched on a hillside. Built over three levels, it had three bathrooms, a kitchen, two reception rooms, an office, three terraces, a garage, garden, covered barbecue area and pool. It was on the market for £318,000. Its particular selling points were its big windows, wonderful views, wooden floors, lots of storage space and an additional small flat, which could be used by visiting friends and family. The kitchen was a tiled shell that they could finish them-

Above: The charms of this nineteenth-century four-bedroom farmhouse didn't outweigh the impracticalities offered by its location.
Below: An impressive designer house would stretch Ben and Amita's budget to the limit.

selves or have the developer complete within the asking price. 'Our initial thoughts were that it was a bit modern with too much construction work going on around it. But it's terribly glamorous and we could see ourselves living there. We loved the pool and outside staircase, the games room and the granny flat.' The location was perfect, being close to the airport, close to Sitges, so Amita wouldn't be too isolated when Ben was away working, and only three minutes away from the International School.

A little way inland, the medieval town of **CANYALLES** shelters between three mountain peaks. Its origins are seen in the architecture, particularly the church and imposing hilltop castle. It remains untouched by tourism and would have offered Ben and Amita the experience of living the slow pace of life associated with the real Spain. Just outside the town stood a four-bedroom rustic farmhouse originally built in 1885 and renovated ten years ago. As always, money goes much further away from the coast and this property was priced at £271,000. It had a vast kitchen with a working bread oven, a large reception room with a raised snug at one end, complete with the original fireplace, unusual antique beds and wardrobes in all four bedrooms. There were two bathrooms, one of which had antique, green tiling. Outside there was a secluded, walled garden and half an acre of land irrigated by the property's own well. Ben and Amita liked it. 'This is really Spanish and just what we're looking for. It's got loads of potential.' It was close to the main road, only twenty minutes away from the International School in Sitges and forty minutes from the airport, but Ben and Amita finally decided they needed to be a little nearer to Sitges.

They went to view a four-bedroom, deluxe, architect-designed villa outside **CUBELLES**, the most southerly resort on the Costa de Garraf. The town's permanent population of 4,000 quadruples during the summer months. Although popular with French and German home buyers, prices tend to be cheaper because of its distance from Barcelona. The hilltop villa had large, light rooms with picture windows giving unbeatable views in all directions. It comprised a living room with a modern fireplace, a large, modern kitchen with lots of cupboards, a master bedroom with a terrace, a substantial granny annexe or children's playroom, and a magical, split-level pool. It had been built just over ten years ago, so the construction warranty had run out. Ben

was concerned about its slightly shabby appearance and agreed that if they decided to make an offer they should insist on a full structural survey. Below the villa there were extensive building works, with a projected seven further villas to be built over the next two years. There was no question about the quality of the outside space, the pool and the views but Ben and Amita felt unsure about the house itself especially because it was over their budget.

Lastly, they visited **PENÉDES** in the heart of Catalonia's wine-producing region, where the undulating countryside and endless vineyards have earned it the name 'Tuscany of Spain'. Here, two farmhouses had been knocked into one modernized, three-bedroom property. Its attractive traditional whitewashed exterior hid a modern interior which retained some of the original features. The particular highlights were the Gaudi-inspired bathroom with a walk-in shower, and the heated pool with electric cover. Ben and Amita appreciated the way it had been so lovingly restored. 'We loved the front of the building with its big barn doors. The owner has a great eye for detail and has been very clever in mixing old with modern elements. But it is too remote for us.'

Ultimately, they decided to see if they could rent the first house they saw for six months before committing themselves. Refused that option, they made an offer which was accepted. It took almost four months for them to sort out the remortgaging of their two properties in England in order to finance the purchase, so they rented an apartment on Sitges seafront until completion. The only fly in the ointment following their move into their new home has been the previous owner's failure to fulfil his promises of making the pool operational, clearing the rubble from the garden and painting the *bodega*. These things were not included in a conditional clause in the contract, but were part of a separate letter. 'We are so happy here and although we've thought we should possibly have been a little tougher at the time and insisted on getting all the work done before moving in, we were advised by our estate agent not to. Both parties have signed the letter

Above: Two farmhouses imaginatively combined and restored into one was, sadly, too far off the beaten track. Below: Exterior and interior views of the villa outside Sitges that Ben and Amita finally bought.

and so we are in a very strong position legally. Hopefully it won't come to that; we'll just have to wait and see.' On the positive side, Jaya has settled into the International School, easily mixing with Spanish, Dutch, German and Australian children, while Amita has made friends after spotting a notice in a shop and joining a yoga class. Ben has been commuting regularly to the UK but is always back home for weekends. Their only sadness comes from missing regular contact with friends and family but otherwise they have no regrets about moving away from the UK.

House hunters

Menorca
Peter and Pamela Gregson

Peter and Pamela Gregson take a break from house-hunting with presenter, Amanda Lamb.
Below: A two-bedroom duplex was available in the exclusive estate of Vista Marina, near Puerto d'Addala.

Menorca is one of the least developed of the Balearic Islands. Situated just off the Mediterranean coast of Spain, it is within easy reach of Barcelona and has its own airport situated near Mahón. Even in the height of summer, it is possible to find a beach to one's self. Unlike its sister, the party isle of Ibiza, Menorca has resorts that are small, sedate and fairly exclusive.

The island has long-standing ties with the British, who occupied it briefly during the eighteenth century and then continued the association when the first charter flight flew there from Britain in 1953. Over recent years, it has become increasingly popular with house hunters, with the result that in some parts of the island prices have doubled within the last three years.

IT consultant, Peter Gregson, and his wife Pamela had decided to sell their Cambridgeshire home to move to somewhere in Lincolnshire in order to be closer to their family, especially their two grandchildren. The sale would release the capital with which they planned to buy a holiday home for the family. They had spent some time searching in mainland Spain but were not keen on what they had found. 'The houses we saw were mainly all on large complexes and not the sort of Spanish villa we're really looking for.' Although prices on the island of Menorca are more expensive than mainland Spain, they were keen to see what would fall within their budget of £120,000.

The first property they visited was on the rugged north-east side of the island. The region is largely undeveloped and much of it is a conservation area, where coves and beaches can only be reached by foot or by boat. A seaside town in the area, Puerto

d'Addala, was once described as 'the most exquisite place on the island'. Today it is no different. The **Vista Marina** is a small, exclusive estate near Puerto d'Addala. Most of its forty-four duplexes had already been sold, but there was a two-bedroom apartment available for £98,000. Set amid the white walls and terracotta walkways, the apartment offered a large, light, open-plan living area with plenty of room for comfortable sofas and cupboard space. It had a compact kitchen with all mod cons except for a dishwasher, although the plumbing was laid on for one. The sizeable master bedroom had a marble-tiled en-suite bathroom and doors leading to a private patio. The house had its own terrace and access to the communal pool. The additional cost to be considered was the community charge, which was not going to be decided by the residents' association until all of the apartments had been taken, although it was unlikely to exceed £300 per annum. If they were at all nervous about the cost, they could console themselves with the knowledge that during high season, the apartment would fetch £500 per week in rent and £300 for the rest of the season. Peter and

Pamela hadn't been keen on the idea of living on a complex, but had this spacious and well-planned option changed their minds? 'I was pleasantly surprised. The kitchen's a bit on the small side but, in a hot country, we would not be doing roast dinners all the time.' They were impressed by the quality of the building and loved the surroundings, but on balance felt that it was slightly on the small side for them.

Money goes much further once you look away from the main resorts. **CIUTADELLA** is the old capital of Menorca, and sprawling renaissance mansions still dominate the old town. After the island's fortunes declined in the eighteenth century, some of these mansions were taken over by farmers who kept their livestock downstairs. Peter and Pamela went to look at one that was close to the thriving market and the old cathedral. This four-bedroom house had an asking price of £119,000. It retained many original features, such as the exposed internal stonework and ceiling beams. It had two bathrooms, a kitchen and a living/dining room with a courtyard and a roof terrace overlooking the town. Because of its position in the historic part of town, there were strict regulations governing any redecoration or renovation. For example, the terrace could not be covered over and any external paint colours had to be approved. It had been stunningly restored and Peter and Pamela were smitten. 'It's a brilliant place full of different turns. Every room was so traditional, it could have been made for us.' The

Above left: A renaissance mansion in Ciutadella was centrally located and benefitted from many original features.
Below: A partially converted two-bedroom townhouse in Mahón was advertised for sale in the local paper.

house was furnished in traditional Spanish oak furniture that Pamela was pleased to hear could be bought for an additional £10,000.

Next, they travelled to the island's current capital, **MAHÓN**, with its three-mile estuary earning it the title of 'Gateway to Menorca.' Mahón is known for its large harbour and for the fact that mayonnaise was invented there. The town had grown under eighteenth-century British rule, when it became a popular retreat for London high society. Nelson is reported to have spent four days there with Lady Hamilton in what is now known as Nelson's house. Just a few minutes' walk from the

harbour was a partially converted two-bedroom town house being advertised privately in the local newspaper for £90,000. It had a large, tiled sitting room with a wood-burning stove and a modern kitchen and dining area. The ground floor was only partially renovated but had a garage, a guest room and hall ready to be adapted to the new owners' requirements. There was also a separate toilet and shower room just off the patio. Peter was doubtful about his abilities in the DIY arena, but was encouraged to hear that there were local grants available to permanent residents in the harbour area. If they bought the place, they would also be saving on an estate agent's commission, thanks to it being a private sale. A private sale does carry an added risk of the deed ownership being suspect, as they may not have been investigated by the legal profession. At any rate, they decided the work that the house needed was more than they wanted to take on.

The sheltered south-east coast of the island is dominated by ancient watchtowers, reminders of long ago when the island suffered regular attacks from its aggressors. Nowadays, the small coves and calm waters make this a perfect spot for young families. With their grandchildren in mind, Peter and Pamela went to look at a new development not far from the fishing village of **ALCAUFAR**. For £144,000, they could apparently buy a plot and build their own detached villa. The show house had two bedrooms with fitted cupboards, a big rustic-style living room, a lovely, square, fitted kitchen, and garden with a patio, barbecue and private pool. In planning their own villa, they just had to keep to the same number of square metres, but could adapt the plans to omit the garage and have a third bedroom or enlarge the kitchen. The agent offered himself as project manager for an additional 3 per cent commission. The Gregsons were unanimous in their reaction. 'We're flabbergasted by it. It's all we ever dreamed of. All we need to know is: Can we afford it?' Peter pressed the agent as to whether the price did in fact include the cost of the land. A cautious man when it comes to spending money abroad, Peter didn't want to settle anything without being absolutely clear as to what they were buying. Finally, after they returned to England, he received an answer. The house cost £144,000, but the land would cost a further £42,000. That, together with the agent's fee and the legal costs brought the amount up to £200,000 plus – almost double Peter and Pamela's original budget.

A new development near Alcaufar offered the possibility of a detached two-bedroom villa.

Since their search for a holiday home began, the Gregsons have settled into their new home in Lincolnshire and become much more involved with their grandchildren. Their priorities have changed slightly, and buying a house in Spain has become a less pressing issue. They do, however, plan to look again on the mainland in the near future, unable to shake off the lure of the Spanish way of life and of their own place in the sun.

House hunters

Costa de la Luz
Lesley Handford and Bob Foad

Taking its name from the luminous quality of light reflected in its clear waters and white-sanded beaches, Costa de la Luz is one of Spain's more undeveloped coastlines. Running the ninety kilometres between Tarifa and Cádiz, it enjoys a mild climate with a constant breeze that blows throughout the hottest summer months. The coast and its hinterland remain remarkably undeveloped, with dozens of traditional white hill-villages, 24,000 acres of nature reserve, and windswept beaches popular with the windsurfing crowd. It is a place of all things Andalucían, including sherry, flamenco music and white horses. The region has been popular with the Spanish for years, but foreign second home buyers are beginning to find their way there too, to the extent that in some areas property prices have risen by 50 per cent with demand outstripping supply.

Lesley Handford and Bob Foad run a pub in Wimbledon and had decided to buy a holiday home in Costa de la Luz. 'We fell in love with the area because it's very Spanish, the people are very friendly, there's plenty of open space and, of course, the beaches.' They were no strangers to the area, having met over a drink in Gibraltar nineteen years earlier, when they were both working there. They had hunted for a place before and would have bought one, but for the fact that their mortgage had not been in place and so they had lost the property they'd wanted. Determined not to make the same mistake twice, they came to search again with a budget of £85,000. They hoped to find a traditional property with character and some land close to the coast.

Bob Foad and Lesley Handford househunt with presenter, Amanda Lamb.

TARIFA is the most southern town in Europe. With miles of clean, windy, white beaches and backed by green, rolling countryside, it is well located. One of the world's top windsurfing locations, it also provides a base for whale- and dolphin-watching excursions. Occupied by the Moors for 600 years of its history, there is still evidence of their presence in the old town with its narrow, cobbled streets and whitewashed houses. Bob and Lesley visited a two-bedroom apartment that was on the market for £72,000. The apartment had been on the market for eight weeks and the owner had already upped the price by £7000. Spanning two sides of a traditional Spanish court-

yard, it was built in the eighteenth century but had been renovated two years ago. It comprised a living room, a kitchen/dining room and a bathroom. The rooms were big and cool with high ceilings, traditional Moroccan tiles, floors and doors. The typically Andalucían patio was cloistered, tiled on the floor and contained lots of potted plants. Both Lesley and Bob were taken with it, appreciating the history of the place, its traditional features and the high level of restoration. Buying here would mean buying into a small community where the neighbours looked out for one another. 'We'd be happy with that because we want to be with Spanish people. That's why we came here and it will help us learn the language.' However, despite loving both the apartment and the town, they decided that, to do it justice, they would need to move there permanently and they didn't feel ready for that.

Further north, past the bog flats and marshlands that dominate the coastline, alongside the particularly dramatic beaches, they came to the village of **SANTI PETRI**. Once a fishing village, it has seen a rush of new building development that is popular with the Spanish who go there for the golf. There, Bob and Lesley saw a three-bedroom house selling at £89,000. The bedrooms were large doubles, the living room was light and airy with a traditional fireplace and dining area. The modern kitchen had a large work surface along three walls. Outside, there was a covered terrace and a garden with plenty of space for a pool. There's no question that, only a mile from the beach, it represented good value for money and Bob and Lesley were pleasantly surprised. The location was ideal and they were encouraged to hear that there was a sizeable green-belt area and also strict, local building regulations which prohibited the development of hotels over three storeys and houses over two. Nonetheless, while appreciating the efforts to retain the quality of the environment, the couple felt that it was further up the coast than they wanted to be.

ZAHARA DE LOS ATÚNES got its name from the tuna fishing community that once lived there but has now found new life as a beach resort. Despite reservations, Bob and Lesley viewed a three-bedroom duplex in a six-month-old complex on the market for £85,000. It had a long, light living room leading out to a balcony, a modern galley kitchen, two pretty, tiled bathrooms, a huge roof terrace looking out towards the Cape of Trafalgar, underground parking and use of a community pool and garden. They were pleasantly surprised by the pleasant and roomy layout as well as the facilities, which included a restaurant, a paddling pool and a children's play area. They would face an annual charge of £350 for the upkeep of the communal areas, though this was likely to be reduced when all 250 properties were complete. The previous year, the town council had responded to local environmentalists by no longer issuing building permits, so the consequent increase in demand for these properties would probably be reflected in the resale price. In the meantime, Bob and Lesley could expect to cover their mortgage by renting the apartment for the three peak summer months for £4–5,000. However, their hearts were set on finding an older property, and so they continued their search.

The white, cliff-top village of **Vejer de la Frontera** is one of the villages that, for hundreds of years, marked the border between Islamic and Christian Spain. Its narrow, cobbled streets, white-walled houses and ruined castle (Alcazár) all recall its Moorish heritage. Becoming more and more popular with foreign buyers, property there is hard to find. However, Bob and Lesley were able to view a two-bedroom apartment in a 200-year-old mansion. The entrance led straight into the kitchen, which had a typically high ceiling and grilles at the windows. The Moroccan feeling continued into the living room. The bathroom was so big the agent had seen people put a table and chairs in there. An added bonus was found in the huge terrace that had so much potential. Legally, it was a communal space, although it was unlikely to be used by the other apartments which all had their own outside spaces. There was nothing pokey about this wonderful apartment but it did need some modernization. 'We've never seen anything like it. We loved the high ceilings, the size of the rooms, the original features and the Moorish feel.' But it was on the small side and didn't have the garden that Lesley wanted so badly.

Above: A three-bedroom duplex in the beach resort of Zahara de los Atúnes. Below: a two-hundred-year-old mansion in Vejer de la Frontera had been converted into spacious apartments.

Seeing these properties and their locations had only strengthened Bob and Lesley's resolve to buy in the region. They have since looked more extensively but have still had no success. They did find a *cortijo* with a large garden near Vejer but sadly the surveyor insisted on by their mortgage lender, the Abbey National offshore, gave it an unfavourable report. So they are back at square one, but their enthusiasm for one day finding a dream holiday home is undimmed.

House hunters

Galicia
Bob Parr and Kay Toon

Above: Bob Parr and Kay Toon with presenter, Amanda Lamb. Below: A secluded three-bedroom stone cottage close to the beach.

The north-west corner of mainland Spain is a far cry from the busy life found on the Mediterranean coast. The region of Galicia offers the possibility of escaping the crowds and establishing a life without a close-knit British community on the doorstep. This is where the Spaniards choose to holiday, drawn by the unspoilt, under-populated landscape offering eucalyptus forests, vineyards, large nature reserves and miles of tranquil waterways. Its dramatic Atlantic coastline is cut by numerous *rias* (estuaries) and boasts as many as 800 beaches, many of which are judged to be the cleanest and emptiest in Spain. The region's major towns are Santiago de Compostela, the impressive end of the road for pilgrims journeying to the shrine of St James, La Coruña, a busy port town, Pontevedra, with its charming medieval centre and Vigo, a hectic town centred around its port. The weather is less reliable than on the ever-popular Costa del Sol but between April and October it can expect to see some regular sunshine. Until recently, property prices were among the lowest in Spain, but with boosted popularity due to the new airport in Santiago, they have risen in some places by as much as a staggering 60 per cent in the last five years.

Bob Parr, chief engineer with the defence industry, and his partner, IT manager, Kay Toon, wanted to escape the stresses of their life in Bedfordshire by acquiring a holiday home in Spain. They had chosen to look in Galicia, 'because we didn't want to go somewhere dominated by tourism but somewhere natural – the real Spain. The idea of its being green, too, really appeals to us'. They were hoping to find a place with character, enough room for friends and family to visit, a good view, a garden and even a vineyard. All of this needed to fall within their budget of £100,000 (including any renovation costs).

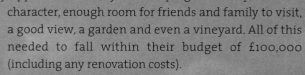

SANXENXO is on a popular stretch of coast. The beaches are crowded in the summer and claimed by the locals to be the sunniest in the region. This stretch of coast is home to a working fleet of fisherman, and oyster and mussel beds are marked by little floating platforms. Prices are still on the increase here, so this might have been a good moment for Bob and Kay to invest. A few minutes' drive into the hills found a restored, three-bedroom, stone cottage with a garden, which had an asking price of £108,000. Set in an idyllic, peaceful location, all the rooms looked out onto spectacular views. The house comprised a kitchen/dining room leading to a comfortable, wooden-ceilinged living room, with bedrooms and a big, cosy attic room upstairs. Bob and Kay were reassured to know that the plots of land in front of the house were all under 20,000 square metres, making it illegal in this area to build on them – so the beautiful views were safe. They liked it. 'It was fantastic. The peace strikes you as soon as you walk up the path and it looks much smaller from the outside.' The property really offered the best of both worlds: it was secluded but only a short distance from the beach. Kay was a little put off, however, by the prospect of having spiders and snakes for company.

Above: A comfortable show house in La Toja demonstrated the potential of buying off-plan.
Below: Pontevedra is typically Galician with graceful squares and narrow streets.

Galicia's most exclusive resort, **LA TOJA** lies on an exclusive, pine-clad islet reached only by bridge. This is something of a mecca for the well-heeled, with a string of hotels, a chic casino and a nine-hole golf course. Its highlight is the small church completely covered in scallop shells, which symbolize successful pilgrimages. Property is in high demand here and finding something to suit Bob and Kay would be difficult. However, there was a new beach-side complex overlooking the bay. It would consist of houses in various different styles, only two of which fell within their budget. The show house was impressive, having four, spacious double bedrooms with tiled floors, two bathrooms, an open-plan living/dining room on two levels opening onto a patio and garden, a fully-equipped kitchen and unfinished attic space big enough for two more rooms. It also had an enormous garage and access to the communal pool and recreation area. It was on the market for £100,000. Bob could see himself restoring vehicles in the garage while the attic could be used as a studio or pool room. The developers had said they would finish the attic for an additional £1000 or, alternatively, Bob and Kay could wait until a later date. A disadvantage of buying off-plan was that it was hard to imagine the final surrounding landscape, particularly since there were individual plots being sold for building right in front of the property. On the plus side, buying now would mean that they would get a lower price. When it was finished, the asking price would be raised by £10,000. They were tempted, but felt that the planned building programme would almost certainly ruin the spectacular views.

The town of **PONTEVEDRA** has some of the most magnificent architecture in Galicia, most notably the granite crosses, built as markers to guide pilgrims. Although it is big enough to support various shops, restaurants and bars, it is also small enough to retain the friendly character of a village. On a hill outside the town was an unusual four-bedroom, modern villa which had a tiled, open-plan living room with two sitting areas, a large kitchen/dining room with a huge window and two bathrooms. There was also a typically Galician, covered terrace, ideal for filling with plants and using as a conservatory, an unusual, wrap-around balcony with

sensational views, a patio with a barbecue, and a garden with fruit trees. The property offered much of what they were looking for, but ultimately they decided that the bedrooms were too small and that they didn't like the design. It was time to look elsewhere.

The province of Pontevedra is an area steeped in history and is the site of one of the most important fortified hill settlements in Spain. This neolithic village was settled in the seventh century and is now one of the most popular tourist attractions in the area. The land here bears the hallmarks of two great Galician traditions: sweeping valleys planted with vineyards, and granite walls marking the endless division of inherited land. Deep in the countryside stood an unmodernized, traditional, three-bedroom farmhouse. On the market for £86,000, it boasted a fantastic wine cellar complete with press, five acres of land including an orchard, a vine trellis, a stable block and two derelict water mills. Two local builders had quoted £14-15,000 to renovate the building completely. Bob had great visions for it, involving putting a bedroom into the roof space and opening the front end up into a huge room with a pitched ceiling. They were both captivated by the place. 'It's an empty canvas with masses of potential. We could make it into something fabulous and we'd have the two watermills so we could get away from each other!' They agreed that there was even the potential of converting the stables to provide a small B & B business.

Above: A modern four-bedroom villa outside Pontevedra with plenty of outside space and spectacular views.
Below: The potential offered by this unmodernised three-bedroom farmhouse was enormous.

When Bob and Kay returned to the UK they discussed at great length how they could buy the farmhouse but sadly concluded that this was not a realistic option as one of them would need to give up their job to oversee the restoration. Splitting up, even temporarily, had not been on their agenda, and so they decided to think again. Convinced that they will achieve a better quality of life in their retirement if they move abroad, Bob and Kay are determined not to give up. They have decided instead to investigate the possibilities in France and on the north-eastern coast of Spain.

Ex-pats

Costa Blanca
John and Fiona Simm

The thought of maintaining a second home often deters people from buying property abroad. However, John and Fiona Simm, who appeared in the first series of *A Place in the Sun*, have found that it is possible with the right support systems. They bought their villa in the *urbanización* of La Sella in 2000. They planned to use it as a holiday home, otherwise lending it to friends or family. Their estate agent introduced them to an English woman, who cleans and keeps an eye on the house when they are not there. 'She's our central contact point and has been an angel. You really do need someone that you can trust because you are so far away. If friends are staying there and something goes wrong, she will sort it out and we transfer any money needed from our Spanish bank account to hers.' They leave the details of a reliable, local English plumber they found through friends, and another Englishman they met through their children looks after the garden, the car and any DIY jobs. The greatest expense is the pool man, who comes weekly throughout the year. His annual £800 charge is lower, however, than the cost of having the pool emptied and refilled. Lastly, the Simms have been lucky with their neighbours who have become firm friends and would always help out if things were desperate.

In fact, the Simms only use their home during the school summer holidays. 'We're limited to our two daughters' term times and we've found the air fares prohibitive at Easter.' Fiona, Giverny and Bronte spend up to six weeks of the summer there with John coming in two or three-week bursts when he can. 'Fiona has made friends with other residents and the girls have a great time mixing with children of different nationalities. As a result, their Spanish is coming along a lot faster than ours. La Sella

Bronte and Giverny Simm enjoy their new home.

The view from the Simm's terrace in La Sella is second to none.

provides everything we need for a holiday – golf, horse-riding and tennis – and the village centre always has something going on in the evening, but we enjoy exploring the surrounding countryside and Valencia. We do enjoy being in such a friendly, summery community and think we might feel too cut off outside it.'

So far they have only had two brushes with Spanish bureaucracy. Once when buying a car that had not been legally registered with the previous owner. 'The paperwork was horrendous and the company holding the papers was only interested in being paid, not in helping me. It was very frustrating to sort out over the phone from the UK.' The second time, John had a kidney stone and was rushed to a private clinic nearby only to find that they did not want to admit him without first seeing his insurance papers or proof of his means of payment. They reluctantly agreed to accept his passport, but then, having admitted and treated him, seemed so determined to keep him there that he had to discharge himself two days later. 'Unnervingly, the clinic was opposite a crematorium and the whole experience convinced me that whether a permanent resident or on holiday, you must be insured.'

The property itself has doubled in value since 2000, so the Simms are planning to add two bedrooms and a bathroom in the underbuild, working with an architect who has worked on similar projects before and is known to their estate agent. Two years on, the pleasure in their dream home is far from dimmed. 'We can't recommend this enough. Our only complaint is that it's a terrible wrench to leave it. We do think of it as home and we miss it when we're not there.'

Ex-pats

Costa Blanca
Pat and Jan Beasley

Buying a property on a whim eventually led freelance journalist Pat Beasley to turn his back on the UK for good. Thanks to a property exhibition in Peterborough in 1985, he went on a four-day inspection trip to the Costa Blanca. He had no intention of buying, but found himself putting down a £500 deposit on a two-bedroom duplex in a small complex in Cabo Roig near Alicante. 'When I got back, I wondered what on earth I'd done, but I was never disappointed. It was only two and a half hours from the UK; the sun shone; I had a little boat and it was cheaper than the south of France.'

Twelve years later, he married Jan at a point when he had reached a watershed in his career. 'I was sixty and working every day of the week when I realized that I didn't want to spend the rest of my life that way. So we bought a three-bedroom house in a complex three miles further down the coast and moved everything. It was a wrench to leave our families but we felt our quality of life would improve. And it did.' The big difference they have found is that they no longer live against the clock. 'I loved working but I didn't realise how stressed I was. The sheer absence of stress is fantastic. We enjoy the climate, eating out, the Spanish attitude towards *mañana* (even though that took some getting used to!) and the fact that your pound goes further here, so we are able to live comfortably.'

Over the next four years, however, life in and around their *urbanización* has changed. 'The traffic and building have got out of control on the coast. In the summer it takes us one and a quarter hours to drive to Torrevieja instead of the usual twenty minutes. Things are more expensive now than when we first came here, but generally it's still cheaper to buy a house and to go out to eat rather than spending hours in the kitchen preparing meals.

'Also there's a well-organized programme of events and activities on this part of the Costa Blanca for ex-pats, e.g. bridge clubs, whist drives, bowls clubs, amateur dramatics and a host of other anglophile interests. That's not our scene, because we like to spread ourselves among the different nationalities over here, not least the Spanish, who, I have to say, are generally very friendly and accommodating.'

Life in an enclosed complex has been enjoyable but they have reached a stage in life where they no longer want to be surrounded

Pat and Jan Beasley lead a relaxed, stress-free existence in the Spanish sun.

by holidaymakers. Their years living there have given them the confidence to try to integrate further into a local community. As a result, they resolved to search for a quieter existence further inland where they would experience something more of the real Spain.

When they saw an old farmhouse being restored

Above right: Jan and Pat Beasley relax in the shade of their new home.
Below: A swimming pool is a must in the heat of the summer.

by a friend, they realized its potential and decided to look for something similar. Having looked at various possibilities which they spotted in local newspapers or found through an agent, they eventually found a renovated *finca* that met all of their requirements. It offered them tranquillity, spaciousness, a taste of the country and yet was only twenty minutes' drive away from the beaches. It had a major drawback, however, in that it was already under offer to some friends. 'We had fallen in love with it. It's restored in the traditional style using reclaimed windows and doors and surrounded by 2,300 square metres of orange and lemon groves and a delightful swimming pool of our own. When our friends baled out, we swooped like birds of prey.' Over two hundred years old, the property has a unique character of its own, with a solarium on the roof that commands spectacular views. Unlike their previous

properties, it came unfurnished so Pat and Jan have taken their time to find furniture that will add to the atmosphere. 'There were no real problems in moving. As in England, you simply find a good solicitor (usually by recommendation) who makes sure you are not being sold a pig in a poke! When I was young I wanted change but I find that at this time of life, the peaceful quality of life here is preferable. The next thing is to get to grips with the Spanish language. I miss being able to sit at a table with Spanish veterans and talk about everyday things. Wild horses wouldn't drag me back to England now.'

Ex-pats

Andalucía
Tony and Christine Martin

Tony and Christine Martin arrived back in London in 1986 after fifteen years of working in the Far East. It was only months before they decided to leave England's grey skies behind and look for a holiday home in southern Spain. 'I knew north-eastern Spain a little but an ex-colleague was working in Andalucía restoring a cork forest, so he was a Spanish-speaking contact who helped us.' They rented a flat for four months in Puerto Sotogrande while they looked for properties. As their search progressed further inland they saw how much more their money could buy. 'We ended up buying the thirty-fourth farm we saw – 123 acres and an uninhabitable ruin – for the same money we'd have spent on a small plot in Sotogrande.' The holiday home forgotten, they decided to build a small hotel instead, renovating and enlarging the ruin and building separate cottages.

Tony and Christine Martin transformed an uninhabitable ruin into their successful hotel, Puerto del Negro.

The purchase itself was trouble-free but they had enormous problems over access. 'The law here is extremely tortuous and it took three years to get access sorted out between the main road and our boundary. Only a matter of seventy metres, but in the end we had to pay a great deal of money to the *señora* next door who owned the land.' The same *señora* had the local concession for electricity and negotiations to install mains electricity took until 1994. Then, mains water became a consideration. 'Until 1997, when we were connected, we'd used decalcified and chlorinated well water. But in 1995, we had a serious drought and had to truck in 33,000 litres of water a week for six months. That was another thing we hadn't budgeted for.'

As the building work began, supervised by a French architect they knew who worked in the area, the Martins rented a house in the nearby white village of Gaucin. The first cottage, intended as the manager's accommodation and office was completed in 1988. The Martins moved in there until the hotel's eventual opening at Christmas 1993. 'Horrendous weather in November 1989 meant we lost everything, including the foundations we'd built for the hotel. Then the exchange control went against us so, because we were using imported sterling, we had to stop and wait until the peseta recovered in 1992, then went flat out.' The main farmhouse was completely rebuilt into a traditional,

white, five-bedroom *cortijo*, including a billiard room, a laundry and storage in the basement, a dining room, kitchen and sitting room on the ground floor with a terrace looking right across the Jimena Valley to Gibraltar.

'It was very easy for us to settle in because there were lots of English living here then and there are more now. The Spanish have not been a problem but understanding the democracy in a small village is more difficult. You don't want to get on the wrong side of the mayor or the doctor.' When they first arrived, neither Tony nor Christine spoke Spanish. 'But it is essential. We learned by listening.' By the time the Portijo Puerto del Negro opened they had tested the market by leasing a house in Gaucín and operating it as a hotel for nine months in 1991. 'Since then, it's all been word of mouth and this place was fully booked when we finally opened.'

The hotel has now been enlarged beyond the *cortijo* to include four, self-catering cottages, all with pools, and a friendly staff of nine, all local. Tony and Christine have drawn on their own travelling experiences to ensure they provide the best welcome possible, resulting in the accolade of being chosen among the Cunard/Tatler *101 Best Hotels in the World*. Their hard work and patience has undoubtedly paid off, and they have come to feel at home in Spain: 'We'd never go back now.'

Italy

Italy

Historically, Italy has been a source of fascination for northern Europeans because of its mixture of the primitive and the sophisticated. The first modern tourists arrived in the seventeenth and eighteenth centuries to marvel at the remains of the Roman Empire – the cradle of European civilization – and at the products of its rebirth in the Renaissance. But, more often than not, they were diverted from history and art upon finding a country of extraordinary charm and diversity, whose seductive climate and sexy, easy-going way of life some saw as dangerous to morals, but many found irresistible. Despite vast economic and social change, these qualities remain a large part of people's attraction to Italy today.

For a millennium and a half after the fall of the Roman Empire, the area was a confused checkerboard of autonomous regions and mini-states, ranging from the powerful, waterborne Republic of Venice to the hotly contested Kingdom of Sicily, with the broad central swathe of the country – the Papal States – ruled by the Pope in a unique, political alliance of God and Mammon. The whole was united, for the first time since the end of the Roman Empire, in 1861. However, in many ways it still resembles a federation of regional states, with widely varying local economies, standards of living, eating habits, wines, architecture and dialects. The topographical spectrum alone ranges from Alpine ski resorts to low-lying alluvial plains, and from dense forests to semi-Saharan desert.

Italy has frequently attracted headlines for its organized crime, political corruption and unstable governments. Yet the nation has thrown itself with gusto into development, first as a secular industrial society and then, since 1980, as a post-industrial service economy and a fully-integrated member of the European Union. It has been remarkably successful. There are great industrial corporations such as Fiat and Pirelli, alongside mega-rich football clubs, fashion and design houses, a multiplicity of television channels and the modern road network. In short, modern Italy is sophisticated and highly diversified, with a population of fifty-seven and a half million who have enjoyed a steady increase in their standard of life. It is a buoyant and optimistic country and its economy is fully in line with that of its European neighbours.

regions

In 1946, Italy was established as a parliamentary republic, with power shared between a government and regional councils chosen by the populace. There are twenty regions in all, each proud of its distinctive characteristics and individual landscapes. Some of the regions have had the same borders for centuries while others, such as Friuli-Venezia-Giulia or Trentino-Alto-Adige, have been established more recently. Having been granted a special statute, these two regions, together with Sicily, Sardinia and the Valle d'Aosta, have greater administrative autonomy than the rest. The differences between the north and the south of the country as a whole are striking: the north is

facts

CAPITAL: Rome
AREA: 301,230 sq km
COASTLINE: 7,600 km
POPULATION: 57,680,000
CURRENCY: Euro
TIME ZONE: GMT + 1 hour
ELECTRICITY: 220 volts
WEIGHTS AND MEASURES: metric
RELIGION: mainly Roman Catholic
LANGUAGE: Italian
GOVERNMENT: Republic
INTERNATIONAL DIALLING CODE: 00 39
INDEPENDENCE: 17 March, 1861
NATIONAL HOLIDAY: Republic Day, 2 June

characterized by its economic dynamism, while the south remains more depressed, with a more relaxed pace of life. On the one hand, there are smart, cosmopolitan towns in tune with the twenty-first century. On the other, there are remote, agricultural communities still existing much as they have for centuries. Here, life stops for the siesta, and an emphasis on the traditions of the Catholic church and the bonds of the family are strongly felt.

Abruzzo

Landscape: wild and mountainous, dropping down to the sandy, Adriatic coastline; castles and hilltop villages

Provinces/major towns: Chieti, L'Aquila, Pescara, Teramo

Highlights: National Parks of Abruzzo, Gran Sasso-Laga and Majella-Morrone, medieval Sulmona, Romanesque churches

Festivals: Snake Charmers' Procession (Cocullo, May), *La Perdonanza* (L'Aquila, October)

Handicrafts: wrought iron and copperware, ceramics, woollen blankets, lace

Food: *maccheroni alla chitarra* (pasta with lamb ragout), *scripelli imbusses* (pancakes in broth), *timballo* (lasagne), *brodetto* (fish soup), *scapace* (marinated fish), local pastries, sugared almonds

Drink: Montepulciano (red wine), Trebbiano (white wine), ratafia (black-cherry liqueur), doppio arancio (orange liqueur)

Basilicata

Landscape: completely mountainous with narrow coastal plains, rich woodland on the border with Calabria

Provinces/major towns: Potenza, Matera

Highlights: cave houses (*sassi*) at Matera, Tyrrhenian coast

Festivals: *Festa della Bruna* (folk festival, Matera, July), Regional Fair of Basilicata (Potenza), *Cavalcata dei Turchi* (Ride of the Turks during the Festa of S. Gerardo (Potenza, May)

Handicrafts: ceramics, wooden goods, fabrics

Food: bread, peperonata, ricotta cheese

Drink: red wines – Aglianico del Vulture, Sangiovese and Montepulciano; white wines – Moscato and Malvasia

Calabria

Landscape: mountainous interior, with villages hugging the hills above the shorelines

Provinces/major towns: Cantazaro, Cosenza, Reggio Calabria

Highlights: hill towns, Byzantine church at Stilo, bronze warriors at Reggio Calabria, Sila Sila plateau

Situated at the head of a sheltered cove, Vernazza is one of Liguria's stunning Cinque Terre villages.

FESTIVALS: Good Friday Procession (Catanzaro, August), *Fiera internazionale agrumaria* (Reggio Calabria, March/April), *Sagra del Folclore* (Reggio di Calabria, September), Sausage Festival (Spilinga, August), Swordfish Festival (Bagnara, July)
HANDICRAFTS: silk shawls, lace, ceramics, woodwork
FOOD: fish soup, stuffed macaroni, spit-roasted kid and pork, *provolone* cheese
DRINK: red wines – Ciro, Pollino and Savuto; white wines – Greco di Bianco, Mantonico di Bianco and Melissa
AIRPORT: Lamezia Terme, near Catanzaro

Campania

LANDSCAPE: mountainous interior, with a fertile coastal plain around Bay of Naples
MAJOR TOWNS/PROVINCES: Avellino, Benevento, Caserta, Naples, Salerno
HIGHLIGHTS: Pompeii, islands of Capri and Ischia, Naples' historic centre, Mount Vesuvius, Royal Palace of Caserta
FESTIVALS: Festival of San Gennaro (Naples, May/September/December), Festival of *Madonna del Carmine* (Naples, July), Festival of *Madonna di Piedigrotta* (Naples, December), Sorrento film festival (Naples, November)
HANDICRAFTS: vietri majolica, crib figures (Naples)
FOOD: *spaghetti alla vongole* (clams), pizza, *calzone* (stuffed pizza), buffalo mozarella
DRINK: red wines – Capri, Gragnano and Taurasi; white wines – Capri, Ischia, Lacryma Cristi, Fiano di Avellino and Greco di Tufo
AIRPORT: Capodichino airport, Naples

Emilia Romagna

LANDSCAPE: mountainous on Tuscan border, but for the most part spectacularly flat with great lagoons in the south
MAJOR TOWNS/PROVINCES: Bologna, Ferrara, Forli, Modena, Piacenza, Parma, Ravenna, Reggio Emilia
HIGHLIGHTS: Bologna's historic centre, Modena's Romanesque cathedral, Parma's medieval baptistery, Ravenna's mosaics
FESTIVALS: Ascension Day Procession (Bologna), *Settimane Estense* (Modena, June/July), *Ferrara Palio* (May), Medieval Parade (Forlimpopoli, September)
HANDICRAFTS: *faenza majolica* (ceramics),

glassware, hand-painted fabrics
FOOD: *pasta alla Bolognese*, parmesan cheese, *prosciutto* (smoked ham), ham, pig's trotters (Modena), pork salami and mortadella (Bologna)
DRINK: red wines – Colli Bolognesi, Gutturnio Colli Piacentini and Sangiovese di Romagna; white wines – Lambrusco, Trebbiano and Bianco di Scandiano
AIRPORT: Guglielmo Marconi, Bologna

Friuli-Venezia-Giulia

LANDSCAPE: alpine country in north, dropping to plains, plateaux and then lagoons and wetlands of the Adriatic coast
PROVINCES/MAJOR TOWNS: Gorizia, Pordenone, Trieste, Udine
HIGHLIGHTS: Romanesque basilica at L'Aquila, Grotta Gigante (outside Trieste), Borgo Castello (Gorizia), Piazza dell Libertà (Udine)
FESTIVALS: *San Rocco* Festival (Gorizia, August), prosciutto festival (San Daniele, August), historical boat pageant (Barbana, July), grape festival (Cormons, September)
HANDICRAFTS: woodwork (furniture, masks, sculpture), ceramics, mosaics, iron and brasswork
FOOD: gnocchi, *bolliti* (boiled meats), *brovade* (sauerkraut), polenta, prosciutto San Daniele
DRINK: red wine – Merlot, Refosco and Grave del Friuli; white wine – Tocai Friuliana, Pinot Bianco and Collio Goriziano
AIRPORTS: Ronchi dei Legionari, Trieste

Lazio

LANDSCAPE: rolling hills north of Rome, more mountainous in the south and east with coastline lapped by the Tyrrhenian sea
PROVINCES/MAJOR TOWNS: Frosinone, Latina, Rieti, Roma, Viterbo
HIGHLIGHTS: historic centre of Rome, the Vatican, Etruscan sites, Viterbo thermal springs, the lakes, hilltop towns of the *castelli romani*
FESTIVALS: *Festa di Noantri* (Rome, July), *Rieti Palio* (July), Flower Carpets Pageant (Genzano, June), jousting and historical parade (Valletri, January)
HANDICRAFTS: leather articles, umbrellas, *zampogna* (bagpipes), lace
FOOD: *stracciatella* (soup), *spaghetti alla carbonara* (creamy sauce), *all'amatriciana*

(hot sauce), *gnocchi alla romana*, *saltimbocca* (veal dish), *carciofi alla romana* (artichokes), cheeses – pecorino, caciotta, ricotta
DRINK: red wines – Olevano, Velletri, Colle Picchioni 'Vigna del Vassallo'; white wines – Frascati, Est Est Est, Marino and Velletri
AIRPORTS: Fiumicino and Ciampino, Rome

Liguria

LANDSCAPE: narrow coastal strip at the foot of mountains terraced for vines and olives
PROVINCES/MAJOR TOWNS: Genoa, Imperia, La Spezia, Savona
HIGHLIGHTS: medieval Genoa, Portofino, the Cinque Terre
FESTIVALS: *Festa della Madonna* (Recco, September), fish festival (Camogli, May), strawberry festival (Casaria Ligure, July), garlic festival (Vessalico, July), medieval games (Giustenice, July)
HANDICRAFTS: ceramics, *mezzari* (traditional Genoese needlework)
FOOD: *farinata* (pancake), *cima* (stuffed veal), pesto, *capon magro* (fish and vegetable salad), razor clam soup, *brusso* cheese, candied fruit, *taggiasca* olives
DRINK: red wine – Rossese; white wines – Cinque Terre, Vermentino and Pigato; dessert wine – Sciacchetrá
AIRPORTS: Genoa; Nice, France

Lombardy

LANDSCAPE: Alps on the border with Switzerland, through the lakes of Como and Maggiore, to the broad plain of the river Po
PROVINCES/MAJOR TOWNS: Bergamo, Brescia, Como, Cremona, Mantua, Milan, Pavia, Sondrio, Varesee
HIGHLIGHTS: Bergamo's historic centre, Certosa di Pavia monastery, Milan cathedral, Bergamo's historic centre, Cremona's campanile, Mantua's Ducal Palace, the Italian lakes
FESTIVALS: *Festa di Sant'Ambrogio* (Milan, December), *Festa di Naviglio* (Milan, June), white truffle festival (Casteggio, November), Frog Pageant (Sartirana, September)
HANDICRAFTS: silk, inlaid woodwork, string instruments, furniture
FOOD: *risotto alla Milanese*, *osso bucco* (knuckle of veal), *cotoletto alla milanese* (veal), *zuppa pavese* (consommé with eggs), *cassoeula* (pork and cabbage), cheeses –

gorgonzola, taleggio, robiola, mascarpone
DRINK: red wine – Valtellina, San Columbano, Oltreò Pavese and Sasselli; white wine – Franciacorta, Valcalepio and Tocai San Martino della Battaglia
AIRPORTS: Malpensa, Milan; Linate, Milan; Bergamo

Marche

LANDSCAPE: rolling countryside dotted with medieval towns and villages, and long, sandy beaches along the Adriatic coast
PROVINCES/MAJOR TOWNS: Ancona, Ascoli Piceno, Macerata, Pesaro
HIGHLIGHTS: Urbino, Grotti di Frasassi, Ascoli Piceno old town, Monti Sibellini
FESTIVALS: *Quintana* (Ascoli Piceno, August), Opera Festival (Macerata, July/August)
HANDICRAFTS: pillow lace, brasswork, musical instruments
FOOD: truffles, *brodetto* (fish stew), *vincisgrassi* (rich lasagne), *stocco all'anconetana* (dried cod)
DRINK: red wine – Rosso del Conero and

Rosso Piceno; white wine – Vernaccia di Serrapetrona, Verdicchio dei Castelli di Jesi and Falerio dei Coli Ascolani
Airport: Ancona

Molise

Landscape: less mountainous and rugged than neighbouring Abruzzo
Provinces/major towns: Campobasso, Isernia
Highlights: Saepinium roman ruins, Europe's oldest village (excavated at Isernia), Byzantine frescoes at Abbazia di San Vicenzo al Volturno, Larino cathedral
Festivals: *Sagra dei Misteri* (Corpus Christi Day, Campobasso), Fair of San Pietro (Isernia, June)
Handicrafts: knives, scissors, lace
Food: mountain cheeses, and lamb, mutton and goat dishes

Piedmonte

Landscape: vast, fertile plains of the Po river surrounded by Alps, includes Lake Maggiore
Provinces/major towns: Alessandria, Asti, Cuneo, Novara, Turin, Vercelli
Highlights: the Turin Shroud, Benedictine Abbey of San Michele
Festivals: wine festivals (Barolo/Asti), Battle of the Oranges (Ivrea, February), Truffle Festival (Alba, October)
Handicrafts: ceramics, hand-made linens, woodwork
Food: *bagna calda* (fondue), *risotto alla piemontese*, *zuppa canavesana* (turnip soup), white truffles, *vitello tonnato* (veal with tuna mayonnaise), *bollito misto in salsa verde* (mixed meats), Turin chocolate
Drink: red wine – Barolo, Barbera, Barbaresco, Gattinara and Nebbiolo; white wine – Cortese, Gavi, Asti Spumante and Moscato; Cinzano, Vermouth
Airport: Turin

Puglia

Landscape: intensely cultivated Tavoliere plain, mountains and forest in the north, with a spectacular coastline, rocky and barren in the south
Provinces/major towns: Bari, Brindisi, Foggia, Lecce, Taranto
Highlights: Romanesque cathedrals,

Frederick II's castles, Trulli region, Grotte di Castellana, Promontorio del Gargano
Festivals: *Disfida* of Barletta (July), *Festa di San Nicola* (Bari, May), *Festival della Valle d'Itria* (Martina Franca, August), Holy Week (Taranto), Octopus Festival (Mola di Bari, July)
Handicrafts: wrought iron and brasswork
Food: pasta with turnip tops, rice and mussels, Taranto oysters, roast kid, delicious pastries
Drink: red wine – Salice Salentino, Brindisi, Copertino and Cacc'è Mmitte; white wine – Locorotondo, San Severo and Martina Franca

Sardinia

Landscape: dramatic, undulating uplands covered in *macchia*, with an attractive, varied coastline
Major towns: Cagliari, Nuoro, Oristano, Sassari
Highlights: Su Naraxi fortress (Barumini), Neptune's Cave (Alghero), Maddalena archipelago, Anghelu ruju cemetery, Nuraghe
Festivals: Feast of the Redeemer (Nuoro, August), Feast of Sant'Efisio (Cagliari)
Handicrafts: ceramics, goldwork, basketry, leather cork and woodwork, tapestries
Food: *malloreddus* (pasta with sausage and tomato), *brodetto* (fish stew), *porceddu* (roast suckling pig), *carasau* bread, pecorino and fiore cheeses
Drink: red wine – Cannonau and Carignano del Sulcis; white wine – Nuragus, Vermintino di Gallura, Vernaccia di Oristano; Mirto liqueur
Airports: Calgiari, Olbia, Alghieri

Sicily

Landscape: excellent beaches; interior typified by hill towns, plains and mountain ranges
Province/major towns: Agrigento, Caltanissetta, Catania, Enna, Messina, Palermo, Ragusa, Syracuse, Trapini
Highlights: Agrigento, Roman villa of Casale, Stromboli, Vulcano and Etna volcanoes, Monreale cathedral, Palermo, Segesta archaeological park, Taormina
Festivals: almond blossom festival (Agrigento, February), Sicilian carriage festival (Taormina, May), Procession of the Mysteries (Trapani), Easter rite at Piana degli Albanesi
Handicrafts: lavaware and earthenware,

The popular thermal spa of Chianciano Terme (Tuscany) is known for the therapeutic powers of its waters.

ceramics, puppets, crib figures, wrought iron
FOOD: seafood, *pasta con le sarde* (sardines), *pasta alla norma* (aubergine, tomatoes ricotta cheese), *tonno alla cipollata* (tuna with onions), grilled swordfish, *cuscusu* (fish soup), *cassata siciliana*, almond pastries
DRINK: red wine – Cerasuola di Vittoria and Corvo; white wine – Alcamo, Corvo and Etna; sweet wine – Malvasia delle Lipari, Marsala and Moscato di Pantelleria
AIRPORTS: Falcone-Borsellino, Palermo; Fontanarossa, Catania

Tuscany

LANDSCAPE: mountains of Alpi Apuane, and rolling, cultivated, pastoral countryside
PROVINCES/MAJOR TOWNS: Arezzo, Florence, Grosseto, Livorno, Lucca, Massa Carrara, Pisa, Pistoia, Siena
HIGHLIGHTS: Florence, medieval Siena, San Gimignano, leaning tower of Pisa, hill towns, Etruscan sites
FESTIVALS: *Scoppio del Carro* (Florence, April), Music Festival (Florence, May), Feast of the Rificolona (Florence, September), Feast of St Ranieri (Pisa, June), Gioco del Ponte (Pisa, June), Saracen's Joust (Arezzo, June), *Palio* (Siena, August)
HANDICRAFTS: leather crafts, straw weaving, ceramics, terracotta, paper, embroidery
FOOD: *ribollita, acqua cotta* (soups), *bistecca fiorentina* (steak), *arista di maiale* (roast pork), *fagioli al fiasco* (beans), *castagnaccio* (chestnut cake)
DRINK: red wine – Chianti, Brunello di Montalcino and Nobile di Montepulciano; white wine – Vernaccia di san Gimignano, Galestro and Parrino; sweet wine – Vin Santo
AIRPORTS: Pisa, Florence

Trentino-Alto-Adige

LANDSCAPE: alpine
PROVINCES/MAJOR TOWNS: Bolzano, Trento
HIGHLIGHTS: Dolomites, lakes and valleys of Brenta Massif, Merano spa, Parco Nazionale dello Stelvio
FESTIVALS: *Festa Vigiliane* (Trentino, June), Polenta Festival (Trentino, September), Habsburg Carnival (Madonna di Campiglio, February), Wine Festival (Merano, November)
HANDICRAFTS: table linen, wood carving, copperwork, weaving

FOOD: *gröstl* (potato and meat pie), *cotto e cren* (ham with horseradish), *canaderli* (dumplings), polenta, mushroom risotto
DRINK: red wine – Merlot, Cabernet, Pinot Nero and Marzemino; white wine – Pinot Bianco, Riesling and Traminer Aromatico del Trentino
AIRPORT: Turin

Umbria

LANDSCAPE: fertile river valley, rolling hills with medieval towns and the Appennines in the north
PROVINCES/MAJOR TOWNS: Perugia, Terni
HIGHLIGHTS: Assisi's Basilica di San Francesco, Perugia, Orvieto cathedral, Todi, Parque Nazionale dei Monti Sibillini
FESTIVALS: Umbria Jazz Festival (July), Spoleto Festival (June/July), Todi Festival (July/August), Candles Race (Gubbio, May), Tulip Festival (Castiglione del Lago, April), Onion Festival (Cannara, September), Calendimaggio (Assisi, May)
HANDICRAFTS: ceramics, enamelware, hand-worked tablecloths, curtains, bedspreads and quilts, lace
FOOD: black truffles, *stringozzi* (pasta), Norcia pork and pork products, spit-roast birds
DRINK: red wine – Colli Altotiberini; white wine – Orvieto, Colli Amerini and Colli Altotiberini
AIRPORT: Pisa

Valle d'Aosta

LANDSCAPE: deep river valley running between the mountains of the Alps
PROVINCE/MAJOR TOWN: Aosta
HIGHLIGHTS: Parco Nazionale del Gran Paradiso, Aosta valley, early Roman sites, Romanesque and gothic castles
FESTIVALS: Bataille de Reines (cow fights, October), historical pageant (Verrès, January), carnival (Courmayeur, February), Apple Festival (Gressan, October)
HANDICRAFTS: wood carvings
FOOD: *carbonada con polenta* (thick beef soup), *calpellineuntze* (cabbage and cheese soup), gnocchi, *fonduta valdostana* (fondue), *trota spaccata* (spiced trout), *riso e castagne* (rice and chestnuts), *salcicce e patate* (sausage and potatoes), *frittata con il salame* (salami omelette)
DRINK: red wine – Valle d'Aosta Chambave

The view across the rooftops of Stresa to Lake Maggiore.

Rouge and Valle d'Aosta Nus Rouge; white wine – Valle d'Aosta Fumin and Valle d'Aosta Blanc de Morgex et de la Salle; sweet wine – Valle d'Aosta Chambave Muscat

Veneto

LANDSCAPE: flat landscape of the Veneto plain contrasts with the breathtaking beauty of the Dolomite mountains and Lake Garda

PROVINCES/MAJOR TOWNS: Belluno, Padua, Rovigno, Treviso, Venice, Verona, Vicenza

HIGHLIGHTS: Venice, Palladio's villas, Roman arena and church of San Zeno Maggiore, Verona, frescoes in Padua

FESTIVALS: Carnevale (Venice, February/March), *Regata Storica* (gondola race, Venice, September), *Venice Biennale* (June/October), *Festa di Sant'Angelo* (Padua, June), Asparagus Festival (Bassano del Grappa, April/May), Fish Festival (Chioggia, July), historical parade (Verona, February)

HANDICRAFTS: wicker- and rattanware, Venetian carnival masks, glassware, paper, lace, ceramics

FOOD: risotto, polenta, *fegato alla veneziana* (liver and onions), *stoccafisso* (dried cod), *brodetto* (fish soup), *tiramisu*

DRINK: red wine – Bardolino, Valpolicella, Merlot and Cabernet; white wine – Soave and Gambellara

AIRPORTS: Marco Polo, Venice; Verona-Villafranca, Verona

Property

When it comes to looking for property in Italy, the attraction of immersing oneself in the Italian culture is often even stronger than those of warm weather and delicious food. Away from the major cities and most popular areas, rural property can still be good value for money and usually offers the possibility of an architecturally attractive home with great character. Property prices in general rise 10 per cent from year to year, although between 2001 and 2002 many places saw an increase of as much as 25 per cent. The most expensive areas are southern and central Tuscany, and in and around the major cities of Rome, Florence, Bologna, Venice and Milan, where apartments in medieval *palazzi* can cost millions of pounds. Nonetheless, there are perfectly affordable properties to be found elsewhere, ranging from apartments and villas by the coast and lakes, to isolated ruins in the depths of the countryside, or terraced homes and cottages in picturesque medieval villages. British buyers tend to stick to the regions north of Abruzzo and Campania. Further south, the summer heat can be stifling, but the landscape is just as stunning and there is no shortage of cultural attractions. Generally, the trend is to head out of the towns (unless work necessitates a base there) and towards the coastlines and lakes, where the high demand can drive

The restoration potential in a traditional Tuscan villa has attracted plenty of people looking for their own place in the sun.

the prices up. Many people opt for the older, traditional country properties, particularly if they have lively areas nearby. Many feel that being within easy reach of a regional town or village, although it costs a little more, represents a better investment.

Central Tuscany, or 'Chiantishire', has been a favourite spot with the British for a long time. Its gently rolling hills are scattered with rough stone farmsteads (*case coloniche*) that have become highly prized by foreign buyers, with the result that prices are high and properties for renovation are extremely hard to find. These buildings are built from local materials, but their style varies, depending on the artistic sensibility of the town they are closest too. Look for differences in the window surrounds, architraves or the arrangement of doors and windows. In medieval times, when neighbouring families were constantly feuding, defensive towers became a distinctive part of the rural landscape. As time went by, these were extended and transformed into landowner's houses, but they remain a prominent feature of the larger country properties. Southern Tuscany is another hot spot for property. Historic towns, such as Siena, Lucca and Grosseto, are popular, with prices rising between 10 and 20 per cent in the last couple of years. However, to the north of the region it is still possible to find affordable, small, derelict farmhouses and village houses.

Also popular is Tuscany's neighbour Umbria, where unrestored farmhouses come a little cheaper. The landscape is less dramatic than Tuscany, and the local architecture similar but in a lighter, local stone. Typical features include large kitchens, bread ovens, *cotto* (red brick) floors, wooden beams and loggias. Hilltop towns such as Todi and Gubbio are popular with many buyers – particularly those who are concerned about the issue of security, as the houses flanking the narrow, cobbled streets are often circled by a defensive wall, their character having been retained over centuries.

Until now, Le Marche has remained sufficiently inaccessible to attract too many buyers. With the advent of budget flights to Ancona, however, and the increase in prices in Tuscany and Umbria, things are changing and demand for property is rising. There are still plenty of dilapidated, white stone country houses and cottages to be found for restoration at reasonable prices. The countryside is reminiscent of Tuscany and there are plenty of small, scenic towns such as Urbino, Ascoli Piceno, Macerata and Pesaro offering idyllic bolt holes from the stresses of an urban life. Here, as in other parts of the country, local authorities keep a sharp eye on development, requiring all restoration to be be carried out in sympathy with the vernacular architecture.

In the north, Liguria, otherwise known as the 'Italian Riviera', has begun to attract interest from foreign buyers. It offers a wide range of locations, from isolated mountain villages with tall, stone houses clustering on hillsides, to expensive villas overlooking the sea. It is perhaps the villas which best characterize this region. Built in the eighteenth and nineteenth centuries, they grace the outskirts of resort towns such as La Spezia, Portofino and Rapallo. Their design depends on nothing more than the whim of the original owner, and so they may be Moorish, Renaissance or even neo-gothic in flavour, with lime-washed stucco façades. Property prices west of Genoa have remained reasonable, while those in the stunning Cinque Terre resorts can be more expensive. The coastal resort of Portofino offers one of the most expensive rows of real estate in Italy.

Property around lakes Como, Maggiore and Garda is also in high demand. The staggering natural beauty and the lake towns, such as Bellagio, Limone sul Garda and Sirmione, have attracted second-home owners from Milan, while its proximity to

Milan airport and to the Swiss and French borders also make it attractive to foreign buyers. Further into the Alps, the region of Valle d'Aosta offers chic ski resorts with solid wooden and stone chalets. A quite different building tradition is found in Emilia Romagna where red bricks (*cotto*) have been used for centuries. They, or terracotta, are often used for additional external decoration. The walls are either left exposed or rendered in stucco and limewashed in the rich earthy colours so often associated with Italian buildings throughout the country – sienna, umber, ochre and turmeric. This is the region that boasts the grandest rural buildings in Italy.

Space allows only a glimpse of the possibilities in store for the would-be Italian home owner. Take care to do the right homework in the region of your choice, don't let the sun go to your head, and a piece of the *dolce vita* could soon be yours.

how to find a property in Italy

As is the case when buying a property anywhere, there is no substitute for visiting the country and looking yourself. However, in the first instance, having chosen the area in which you want to concentrate your search, look in magazines such as *World of Property* or *Homes Overseas*. There are fewer agents in the UK who specialize in selling Italian properties compared with those dealing with Spain or France, but they can be found through their advertisements in magazines or national newspapers. They may also have stands at the international property exhibitions throughout the UK. FOPDAC (Federation of Overseas Property Developers and Consultants) can provide a list of agents registered with them. The Net is another source of agents both in the UK and Italy.

For your own protection, if looking through Italian estate agents (*immobiliari*) it is advisable to use one that is registered with the local Chamber of Commerce (they should have a certificate as proof). Check that your agent has indemnity cover. They should also be a member of either the AICI (*Agenzia Immobiliare Centro Italia*)or FIAIP (*Federazione Italiana Agenti Immobiliari Professionali*). Agents fees vary and are payable by the buyer, by the vendor or split between them. As everywhere, there are good and bad agents. A good one, who is familiar with the laws and tax systems of both countries, will help you through the purchase, from drawing up the preliminary contract (see below) and providing you with a translation, right through to making sure the mains services are registered in your name and switched on.

Liguria's hilltop town of Apricale is one of the many tempting possibilities for the home buyer wanting to get away from it all.

How to buy a property in Italy

Italian law does go a long way to protect foreign property buyers but, as with every country, it is advisable to seek your own independent legal advice before you sign anything or transfer money. This basic guide will give you an idea of the process.

Having found the property, but before signing the preliminary contract (*compromesso*), you will need to conduct a survey, local searches, and a check as to whether the property conforms with local planning and building regulations. Properties in Italy are not automatically surveyed before a purchase. However, for your own peace of mind, it is wise to appoint an architect/surveyor (*geometra*) who will not only be able to survey the property and provide you with a written report, but can also plan any alterations with you, submitting them for approval and overseeing the work.

The preliminary contract (*compromesso*) can be drawn up by the vendor, the estate agent, a notary or a lawyer. This document should include the terms of the sale: details of the property, the seller and buyer, the price, how the purchase will be financed, completion date, and details of any other conditions (such as the buyer being able to obtain a mortgage or planning permission, or the discovery of local plans to build something that will affect the property) that have to be completed before the sale. At this stage a deposit (*caparra* or *deposito*) of anything between 10 and 30 per cent is payable to the vendor. Make sure you are absolutely clear about the terms of the deposit and whether and under what circumstances it might be returned.

It is possible to register the *compromesso* with the local registration tax office. This has the advantage of preventing another prospective buyer getting involved because they will be informed of the existence of your *compromesso* when they conduct local searches. You will need to make sure that the property is still in the condition you saw it when you made your original offer and includes everything you agreed to buy. Make a visit with your lawyer to check. Consult your lawyer and/or estate agent about the declaration of value, which is normally less than the purchase price and is set by the local registry and *comune*.

By the time you are ready to complete, you must have fulfilled all the conditions in the contract and obtained an Italian Tax Code Number (*codice fiscale*). Completion must take

The rolling Tuscan countryside continues to be a favourite destination for British home buyers.

The original features found in many traditional Tuscan buildings contribute character and charm to a home.

place in front of a notary (*notaio*). A notary is an independent representative of the government who has the authority to transfer legal title to properties, and is appointed and paid for by the buyer. If the buyer is not fluent in Italian then an officially accredited interpreter must be present, or alternatively, the buyer must give power of attorney to his lawyer or estate agent. Before signing, the balance of money payable by the buyer (including the notary's fee and any relevant taxes) must be presented, preferably in the form of a banker's draft. After signing, the property is yours.

All that remains is for the notary to register the change of ownership at the land registry. The buyer should collect a copy of the purchase deed from the notary's office a couple of weeks later. The notary will provide the buyer with a form with which to notify the local police of the purchase. After this, you should contact the mains suppliers, notifying them of the change in the property's ownership, and then you can sit back and enjoy it.

planning permission

This is granted by the *comune* (local council) who will inevitably set restrictions on the restoration of a historical building. Their primary concern is to protect the environment. This means, for example, that the original style of the building will have to be respected: you may be unable to extend a building beyond the footprint of the original; there may be difficulties in adding or siting a swimming pool; and there may be restrictions on changes to the exterior of a town house. Building from scratch is relatively rare, but if you are considering buying a plot, check first that it is not designated farming land and be prepared for an inordinate amount of red tape before you get planning permission. The agency selling the land should be able to help you.

grants

These are the gift of the local council and do exist for listed buildings. However, it is a laborious business applying for one and they are by no means guaranteed, with the result that few people bother. If buying, it is better to rely on raising sufficient funds yourself.

mortgages

The most straightforward way to finance the purchase of your new home is through the sale of your previous one, or by remortgaging the house you already own. This puts you in the advantageous position of being a cash buyer. If necessary, mortgages can be arranged through Italian banks but they are expensive and may take some time to be approved. The maximum loan is 85 per cent, but this is only available to residents. Second homeowners will probably only be able to borrow up to 50 to 60 per cent. It is worth both shopping around and haggling to find the most advantageous terms. Repayments are usually made over ten or fifteen years. Italian lenders do not always survey the property, but will often accept the official fiscal value and take a first charge on the property. There are now also a number of international branches of British banks and building societies in Italy who will arrange mortgages. To obtain a mortgage, you will need to provide details of your financial situation and be prepared to pay the various arrangement costs.

insurance

It is not a legal requirement but it is a wise precaution to take out household insurance to cover all eventualities – third party, theft and damage. Read the small print carefully to make sure there are no loopholes, particularly if it is a holiday home, where you may be penalized for long periods of absence or inadequate security.

inheritance law

Seaside resorts like Porto Ercole provide ideal holiday homes for families with young children.

As in France, Spain and Portugal, inheritance law in Italy is a complicated subject and taking professional advice is recommended. Like the law in those aforementioned countries, Italian inheritance law dictates that the children of the deceased have an inalienable right to fixed shares of the property. If you buy the property through a company you will avoid the inheritance laws, although you should take legal advice on the longer term pros and cons. Otherwise, it is simplest to draw up an Italian will stating you wish to leave the property according to the laws of your own country.

A public will (*testamento pubblico*) is the most secure and is drawn up by a notary (*notaio*) and signed in front of two witnesses. Rarely used is the secret will (*testamento segreto*) which is handed to the notary in a sealed envelope. Frequently used is the holographic will (*testamento olografo*), handwritten, signed and dated by you. This is convenient but can invite legal problems if thought to be forged.

Living in Italy

residency

EU nationals can stay in Italy for 90 days or an indefinite period provided that they have a resident's certificate. Apply for a *certificato di residenza* (certificate of residence) through the local *comune* (town hall).

fiscal code

All Italian residents require a fiscal code. It can be obtained at the local tax office (*intendenza di finanza*) and is necessary for buying property, paying bills and opening a bank account, among other things.

work

An EU national can work in any other member country without a work permit. However, you may be asked to apply for a *libretto di lavoro* (work registration card). This can only be acquired through the local *comune* (town hall) after you have received your *certificato di residenza*.

If proposing to move to Italy permanently and work for a living, do not underestimate the difficulties of obtaining a job, unless you have arranged something before moving. Your Italian may need to be fluent to convince a potential employer that you are a better bet than an Italian competing for the same job. If planning to set up a business of your own, take care to investigate the detail thoroughly and provide for all the pitfalls that may occur, including not being granted a residence permit. The bureaucracy involved will be complex and frustrating.

social security

Italy has a social security system similar to that of the UK, although contributions are relatively higher. The system covers employed and self-employed individuals while others can register voluntarily. Consult leaflet SA29 (from the DSS) for details of social security, pension rights and healthcare within the EU.

pensions

If retiring to Italy, it is a wise precaution to take some pension planning advice. Pensioners are entitled to receive their UK state pension, receiving the annual increases and Christmas bonus. If you are an Italian resident then you must declare any private pension as part of you world-wide assets and pay Italian tax on it. If you have already paid UK tax on it, you can claim to have it refunded or set against the Italian tax due.

bank account

If you are living and working in Italy, it will be necessary to open a bank account.

government

Italy is a republic headed by a President, who is elected for a seven-year term with a bi-cameral Parliament. The Parliament consists of the Chamber of Deputies and the Senate, both elected by universal suffrage. Both chambers have similar functions, with neither one taking precedence over the other. The country is divided into twenty *regioni* (regions). For historical reasons, five regions – Friuli-Venezia Giulia, Valle d'Aosta, Trentino Alto-Adige, Sicily, Sardinia – have been granted special semi-autonomous or autonomous powers. The remaining fifteen each elects a *consiglio regionale* (council) every four years. This forms a *giunta regionale* (local government) that has limited financial, legislative and administrative powers that are exercised within the bounds of laws passed at national level. The regions are subdivided into ninety-six *province* (provinces) that are in turn split into *comuni* (town councils) that administer local services.

pets

There are no quarantine procedures, but you will have to provide an international health certificate signed by a vet who is registered with the Ministry of Agriculture. The certificate should be issued no more than two weeks before departure. If you want to take your animal back into the UK, you must get a pet passport.

Talk to other expatriates to find out which bank they would recommend. You may need to produce your *residenza* before being issued with a chequebook and guarantee card. It is illegal to write a cheque if you have insufficient funds in your bank. Bank charges are high, so many people retain a UK account, transferring the minimum amount necessary.

taxes

The Italian taxation system is fiendishly complicated and best tackled with the help of expert financial advice from an accountant (*commercialista*). Tax evasion is rife in Italy but the penalties when caught are high. Regulations frequently change, so this introduction is designed only to give you an idea of the sort of thing to expect. Italy has a double tax treaty with the UK.

INCOME TAX: If you spend over 183 days in Italy or are considered to be tax resident, then you will be classified as a resident and liable to pay Italian income tax (*Imposta sul Reddito delle Persone Fisiche*/IRPEF) on your worldwide income, both earned and unearned. Unless you are paid by PAYE, or are exempt from paying tax, you will be responsible for registering yourself at the local tax office (*Intendenza di Finanza*) and filling in tax returns. Unlike the UK Inland Revenue, they will not chase you but expect you to fulfil your own obligations unaided. Taxes range from 19 per cent to a punitive 46 per cent. The tax year runs with the calendar year, and returns are due between May and June, with heavy penalties incurred for late payment. All property owners must pay tax on rental income, whether the money is received in Italy or abroad.

The charms of medieval towns such as Tuscany's Massa Maritama never wear thin for those attracted to the relaxed pace of Italian life.

Equally, all property owners are liable to pay income tax based on the notional letting value of the property. This is a fixed percentage of the official value (*valore catastale*).

COUNCIL TAX: All property owners pay a council tax (*Imposta Comunale sugli Immobili*/ICI) in two instalments a year, based on the property's declared value. The rate is fixed and collected by each local *comune* (council).

CAPITAL GAINS TAX: There is no capital gains tax in most cases.

INHERITANCE TAX: Residents and non-residents are subject to inheritance tax if they own property in Italy. The tax varies according to the relationship between the deceased and the beneficiaries and, although taxed separately, must be declared as part of an individual's income.

VAT: The ordinary rate is 20 per cent.

GARBAGE TAX: A garbage tax (*tassa sui rifiuti solidi urbani*/TARSU) must be paid to cover rubbish collection.

education

Education in Italy is compulsory between the ages of six and fifteen. The Italians have always prided themselves on their rigorous, classically-based system, although there are plans underway to radically overhaul it, in order to create a more flexible system and bring it into line with the rest of the European Union. However, at the time of writing the system remains unchanged, with five years of primary education in a *scuola elementare* (primary school*)*, followed by three years in the *scuola media* (lower secondary school) at the end of which successful students receive a *Diploma di Licenza di Scuola Media* and with it the right to continue their education. At this point, the student chooses a more specialized course, for example, classics, science, arts, teacher-training, or vocational or technology-based courses. At the end of five more years of schooling, the successful student receives a *Diploma di Maturità*, which grants admission to those faculties in Italian universities not requiring any additional entrance examination. Altogether, there are forty-two state universities in Italy, three technical universities (*politecnici*), six non-state universities and eleven university institutes (*istituti*) which are regulated by special statutes, as well as numerous foreign programmes (there are thirty-two American colleges in Florence alone).

To find out which schools are local to you, visit the *comune* (town hall). Visit the ones that you think may be right for your child and, if possible, talk to other parents with children at the school. Unlike the UK or France, you are not limited to those within

Distinctive white square houses with Moorish influences distinguish Positano, one of the most popular resorts on the Amalfi coast.

furniture and goods

If establishing a permanent residence in Italy, you can normally transport any furniture and goods into the country free of customs duties, as long as you are an EU national.

your catchment area but are free to apply wherever you choose.

Foreigners moving to Italy with older children may prefer to take advantage of one of the international schools working for an American, English or international qualification. Fees are high but class numbers tend to be low. The education department of the Embassy will provide a list of the schools in the major towns.

healthcare

Italy has a national health service (*Servizio Sanitario Nazionale*/SSN), entitling residents paying social security contributions to low-cost healthcare. To sign up with a doctor, go to the *Azienda* or *Unita Sanitaria Locale* (USL) office to be registered with the SSN. You will be given a national health number, a health card and a list of doctors with whom you may register. If you have children under six, you will be given a list of paediatricians too. For minor complaints, go to the local *farmacia* (chemist) who will almost certainly be able to help you. For hospital admission you will need a doctor's referral unless it is an emergency.

The Italian health service, like the NHS, has been criticized for its long waiting lists at hospitals, with the result that many residents are privately insured. Non-residents should have an E111 (from their local post office in the UK) entitling them to free emergency treatment while in Italy as a tourist. Normally, you will pay the doctor and reclaim the fees as directed on the E111 form. Taking out extra insurance cover is also recommended.

Dental treatment and treatment by opticians are not always covered by the health service. If moving permanently, an E106 form (from the DSS) gives British nationals reciprocal health cover for two years after a move abroad.

mains services

ELECTRICITY: Most electricity is supplied by ENEL (*Ente Nazionale per l'Energia Elettrica*). When buying a new property, check that all previous bills have been paid and sign a new contract at the local ENEL office. You will need to provide them with the necessary documentation, including your foreign address or that of a representative in Italy who will be responsible for paying your bills every couple of months. An estate agent worth his salt will be able to sort all this out for you.

GAS: Gas is supplied by ITALGAS or SIG (*Societa Italiana per il Gas*) or by a regional company. Although widely used in the north of the country, gas is not available further south or in the countryside. Contact ITALGAS to sign a contract. The conditions are similar to those agreed to when contracting for electricity. Bottled gas is common for cooking and heating in rural areas and for heating in towns and cities.

WATER: Water is supplied locally by the *comune* which will have its own regulations concerning use. If you are living in the south, the area may be subject to severe water shortages during the summer. Rural properties may have wells, but before buying the property, check that yours is reliable and not prone to drying out. Alternatively, it is possible to install a tank that can be filled by tanker, although this is a rather expensive solution.

cars

A foreign car can be imported, providing it has been registered in the owner's name for over six months or its mileage is over 6,000 km. After checking the car through customs, residents can drive using foreign plates for a year before they have to register the car in Italy. Non-residents can drive on a foreign plates and registrations for one year. EU residents can use their existing pink licence until registering the car, when, in theory, the licence should be re-registered as an Italian licence.

House hunters

Puglia
Dessa Gilchrist

Puglia is the heel of Italy, lapped both by the Adriatic and Ionian seas. Strategically placed, it has been occupied over the centuries by almost every major power, each of whom have left their mark, evident for instance in the Saracen old quarters found in many towns, the Norman cathedrals, such as those in Bari, Barletta and Trani, or the Spanish Baroque architecture in Lecce or Martina Franca. There are four geographical regions: Gargano in the north, considered by many to be the most attractive part of the region with its wooded hills and rocky coastline; the Tavoliere, a flat, fertile growing area for the durum wheat that makes Italian pasta; the Murge, vibrant green plains southwest of the region's capital Bari; and Salento, the barren peninsula in the south. Five hundred miles of sandy and rocky coastlines enjoy a warm, dry climate and attract a growing number of tourists. The people here are kind and open with their own regional cuisine, good wines, and numerous religious and popular festivals.

Dessa Gilchrist is in love with Italy. 'I have been everywhere in Italy and I haven't found a square metre that I didn't like. It may be because it is similar to my home country of Yugoslavia, but all I know is that as soon as I set foot in it, I feel different.' Dessa's family is English and they love England, but she would like to spend some months of the year somewhere warmer. She had looked for a second home in Tuscany, but realized that her money would go further in other parts of the country. She was looking for somewhere with a large kitchen and herb garden, which would have enough space to accommodate her family and friends. This was her first visit to Puglia and she was keen to see what her budget of £60,000 could buy.

Above top: A nineteenth-century townhouse in Ostuni offered great views across the rooftops of the town. Above: Exposed stone walls added character to the living room.

OSTUNI is a beautiful, small town just to the west of the shipping port of Brindisi. Originally it was situated by the sea, but its inhabitants felt vulnerable to attack, and so, in the eleventh century they moved four miles inland, establishing the present town on three neighbouring hills. The town centre occupies the highest of the three hills and is known for its gleaming-white buildings and cobbled streets. It has a reputation for having the longest-living residents in the whole of Italy.

In the historic centre of this town, there was a three-bedroom, nineteenth-century townhouse being sold for £55,000. It had started off as two buildings, but together they offered a tiled, stone-walled living room, a small but efficient kitchen, a charming master bedroom with unusual stone arches reminiscent of a medieval church, and a second, good-sized bedroom of a quite different character. The icing on the cake was the roof terrace, which commanded a splendid view across the rooftops. The rental potential on this property was good, estimated at £1,000 a month during the summer, dropping to £350 a month in the winter. Dessa liked what she saw. 'I love the house, the low ceilings, the beams, and especially the terrace, which leads off one of the kitchens.' If she was going to take things further, it was important to check the deeds carefully. Until 1967 Italian houses did not have deeds, but after this date they were granted them in retrospect. The fact that this house had originally been two separate buildings meant that it was doubly worth checking for any possible complications. However, Dessa decided that her heart was in fact set on finding a place in the countryside.

Martina Franca is a walled city founded over 1,000 years ago by refugees from the Saracens. It has been a prosperous town since medieval times, with monuments and buildings reflecting different periods of success, including a gothic church and various Rococo and Baroque buildings. Every summer a music festival is held there, featuring outdoor operas and orchestras. Just outside town, there was a small cottage converted from a seventeenth-century outbuilding that had been used for pressing wine. It had been recently restored, retaining many of its original features and had an asking price of just £20,000. Inside, there were two, separate, well-proportioned flats, each with a reception room, one bedroom (containing the only windows in the place), a shower and basic kitchen. It stood in half an acre of land and had foundations ready for a verandah and barbecue. 'From the outside it's deceptive. But the rooms are reasonably sized with lots of potential. Much could be done with it, especially outside, where you could have an orchard or olive grove.' Indeed, there were plenty of

Below: A seventeenth-century outbuilding converted into two one-bedroom flats offered plenty of potential for renovation.
Below bottom: Trulli, white-washed farmhouses with conical turrets, are unique to Puglia.

possibilities, such as building mezzanine sleeping areas beneath the tall ceilings, adding a roof terrace, or knocking through the reception rooms to create one, big living room. Whatever her plans, they would need to be carried out with the aid of a *geometra*, who would act as surveyor, architect and builder, assessing, planning and pricing any work that was to be done. Although an interesting proposition, Dessa thought that it was too small for her, her friends and family.

A slow, peaceful way of life awaits in the **Valle d'Itria**, dotted with oak saplings, fruit trees and vineyards. This is where the unique *trulli* are to be found, small farmhouses with conical turrets which date from the fourth century, when the number of turrets on the house were an indication of wealth. Fully renovated *trulli* rarely come onto the market and when they do, they're not cheap. Dessa could not resist looking at one, even though, at £93,000, it was way over her budget. The white two-turretted house set in one and a half acres of land included two airy bedrooms, two bathrooms, a modern kitchen with a view, and a large open-plan living/dining room which occupied the original *trulli* and featured the original arches, whitewashed stone and an elegant, semicircular window. The place had so much character, Dessa was overwhelmed by it. 'It's magic. It lived up to my expectations completely. The inside opens up beautifully. The arches and windows are so harmonious.' Every detail had been considered. The price had been dropped from £101,000, which had included all the furniture. Dessa felt that although she liked the décor, she would want the owners to take the things they loved with them, leaving her the rest. Another consideration was the fact that grants could be had from the local council for maintenance work. However, these were offered on a first come, first served basis, so any owner would have to move quickly when they came up. 'What a dream. If it was just me, I'd jump at it. But I want to be able to accommodate my family and friends comfortably, so that they can enjoy the area and everything else that goes with it. So this, sadly, is too small for that.'

The Puglian countryside inland and south of **BARI** is regularly cooled by a gentle breeze, making it an ideal place to escape the heat of the coastal plain. Many Italians own second homes here, the most prized of which are the *masserie* (old farmhouses). It is rare for a renovated *masserie* to come on the market, but Dessa was fortunate enough to find a 200-year-old, four-bedroom manor house with an asking price of £59,000. The interior was light and open, with a living room and kitchen, a bathroom and roof terrace. The property had

Above top: The well-restored trulli proved to be Dessa Gilchrist's idea of a magical, dream house.

Above: Renovated masserie (farmhouses) provide spacious accomodation but rarely come onto the property market.

two acres of land with almond, plum and cherry trees, an outbuilding, stables and traditional bread ovens. Dessa loved the house, its position and surroundings, 'There's enough space for my whole family and friends, and lots of cooking space, which is very important to me. I was surprised and delighted to find the original pizza ovens so I can cook them the real Italian way.' She was undaunted by having to maintain the garden, though relieved that local farmers offered to tend to it in her absence in exchange for fruit from her orchards. A possible hiccup in a purchase could be because of the deeds. A local notary advised that they would have to be reissued, on the basis that a previous notary had not been sufficiently thorough. The bureaucracy involved could take some time, but Dessa was adamant that she was happy to wait.

When she returned to England and presented the details to her husband and three sons, they were less convinced, wanting her to be somewhere with mains water and closer to the sea and basic facilities. 'I could feel that they were not ready for me to make the move yet.' Dessa had thought she might buy the *masserie* with a friend, but when they were asked to make an offer within three or four weeks because of other interest, they decided they didn't want to rush things. So, allowing fate to intervene, they let it go. 'I was disappointed because I had been living there in my mind, imagining all the things I would do. But now I will carry on searching for something that my family will like more. We will have to find a compromise because, unlike them, I want the peace and quiet of somewhere remote. My husband isn't interested in buying property abroad, but eventually I will find the perfect summer home in Puglia.'

House hunters

Le Marche
Susanne and Justin Finden-Crofts

Above: Fields of sunflowers in Le Marche.
Below: The historic town of Serra San Quirico offered a three-bedroom townhouse with parts dating back to the thirteenth century.

Still unspoilt by tourism, Le Marche lies on the east of central Italy, flanked by the Adriatic Sea and the Apennine mountains. The beaches may be busy but inland, life goes on as it has for centuries within the picturesque villages set high above the wooded valleys and rolling fields. The area contains some of the most spectacular mountain scenery in Italy, with protected national forests shrouded in medieval legend. Its capital, Ancona, is a busy sea port, while further inland, towns established during the Renaissance period are still home to historic palaces, castles and museums. The jewel in the crown of these is Urbino, an atmospheric town established in the fifteenth century. Le Marche has the same Italian lifestyle and weather as Umbria or Tuscany, but far fewer British inhabitants. It boasts better beaches and lower house prices than neighbouring Tuscany, although the prices have doubled within the last decade. Those thinking that Italy might be too expensive for a second home may still be pleasantly surprised.

Buying, doing up and selling houses on has been Susanne and Justin Finden-Crofts' stock-in-trade in the UK since they first met. They longed for long, lazy summer holidays and for some time had been dreaming of owning their own holiday home in Italy. 'I[Justin] first came into contact with Italy fifteen years ago, through studying classical sculpture, and I fell in love with the place. We have reached a point when we can afford to invest in a second home, and Italy has everything we're after: long, warm summers and a beautiful, unspoilt landscape; quality, fresh produce for home cooking, combined with superb, friendly, local restaurants for dining out. And, of

course, its unique style and culture.' They were hoping to find a property that would need some renovation with a little land, which was easy to reach from the UK. Their search began in the peaceful, medieval town of **SERRA SAN QUIRICO**. Thick fortifications date back 700 years, providing covered walkways and alleys to protect the inhabitants. Because of the many wars fought in the region, many houses have caverns beneath them for storing provisions and water. Today, the town is famously hospitable and Justin and Susanne were lucky to find a restored three-bedroom town house with parts dating back to the thirteenth century, which was on the market for £81,000. It occupied four storeys, spanning

Left: A deconsecrated church and adjoining priest's house would make a house with a difference.

Above: The church contained Baroque frescoes painted by travelling artists.

Below: A sympathetically converted farmhouse in the Camerino proved too isolated for the Finden-Crofts.

two street levels and comprised a light, modern living room with windows looking out to the countryside, a massive kitchen with a long dining area and fireplace, and two bathrooms including a huge shower. 'It was a superb house. The layout was good, the views were spectacular and we loved the town, its history and the friendly people.' They were untroubled by the stipulation that the exterior of the building had to remain as it was to keep the historic centre intact but, despite loving the building, they decided to hold out for somewhere with some outside space.

The **SIBILLINI** mountains are the legendary home of the God Apollo and Goddess Sibyl who allegedly lived in a cave with her coven, tempting local men into the hills, never to return. The main route for pilgrims wending their way to Rome winds through hills and forests, and the whole area has become popular with hikers and ramblers. In this area of spectacular beauty stood a deconsecrated fifteenth-century church on the ancient pilgrims' path to Loretto. The church itself contained some fine frescos from the Baroque period, painted by travelling artists. Among them was a fine centrepiece, showing the angels transporting Mary's house from Nazareth to Loretto. The other notable features were the magnificent trumpet pillars behind the altar. Just off the church was a vestry, with elegant buttressed arches and a font. The priests' house contained two bedrooms, a spacious kitchen with a large, original fireplace, a basic bathroom, and a garden with views of the mountains. The owner was asking £75,000 for the lot. It would be a massive renovation job, which could be done in two parts, starting with the priests' house. The foundations would have to be reinforced due to an earthquake in 1997, even before the renovation could begin. A government grant for restoring the ceiling could cover as much as 50 per cent of the cost, but they would have to make it available for the public to see by

appointment. 'To restore it to its former glory would be a labour of love, and we're not the people to do it.'

Next, they visited the rich farmland of **CAMARINO**, a patchwork of fields, pasture, woodland, lakes and reservoirs. Although it is not near the coast, there are plenty of places in which to fish, swim or laze by the water. They visited a four-bedroom farmhouse, pleasantly off the beaten track and converted only seven months earlier to include a self-contained apartment. It consisted of two living rooms, two kitchen/dining rooms (one converted from the old cattle stable, which had a marble-topped island and plenty of open shelves), two bathrooms, a stable block and a large, south-facing garden. 'It's exactly what we expected an Italian country house to look like – the brickwork, the colours of the house, the area, the views – it's lovely. The architect has been very sympathetic to the original, without being over-elaborate and there's still a bit for us to do.' Part of that bit would be to add a pool at an estimated cost of £8,000. This wonderfully tranquil, secluded hideaway had an asking price of £124,000. Given that local architects and builders estimated restoration costs at £450 per square metre, making an estimate on this house of £220,000, it looked a bargain. But, sadly for Justin and Susanne, it was just too isolated for convenient commuting to the UK.

The beaches on the Cornero Riviera get very crowded in the high season, but only fifteen minutes inland Justin and Susanne discovered the beautiful village of **OSIMO**. A converted, 1930s accordion factory offered three downstairs bedrooms, a living room and dining room, both done out in English style, a sizable, well-equipped, modern kitchen, a striking blue-and-white tiled bathroom, a studio (its tartan carpet inspired by a Scottish pub) and garages. The asking price was £202,000. The bedrooms were designated on the deeds as storage space, rather than habitable living areas. The reason for this was that Italians pay council tax based on the number of square metres of living space, so the owners were saving themselves approximately £100 per year. Whoever bought the house would be wise to specify that the rooms be redesignated as a condition of sale. The only outside space was a balcony, although there was a plot below belonging to the house next door, apparently the subject of a family feud that was promising to resolve itself. If the feud was resolved, the land might be available for purchase. But although the Finden-Crofts loved the region – 'Unspoiled, undiscovered – it's the perfect place for us' – they weren't sufficiently inspired by this property to want to make an offer.

On returning home, Justin and Susanne saw that the visit had crystallized their thoughts. Although they had originally envisaged buying a property like the farmhouse, they realised that their current work commitments in the UK would make it difficult to visit often enough, making them constantly worried about its security. Instead, they have decided to return to the area to find a village house with some outdoor space, however small, that they will then sell after a year or so. By that time, they intend to have arranged their work so that they can spend more time in Italy and justify buying their ideal farmhouse.

Above top: A converted accordion factory offered airy modern accomodation but little outside space.
Above: The interior had been renovated sympathetically to provide comfortable open-plan living.

Ex-pats

Bologna, Italy
Sonia Coady and Graham Ditchfield

Even though language consultants Sonia Coady and her husband Graham Ditchfield had lived in Bologna for some years and did very careful research before buying a property, the experience was not all plain sailing. 'You read fairytale versions in books, but it's different if you're trying to live and work here. You want efficiency, not charming or eccentric characters to put in a book.'

Sonia arrived in Bologna in 1992, having worked there as an au-pair in her university vacations. 'I came back for a couple of years because I wanted to get my Italian up to speed but then I got sucked into Bologna and never left. It's got most of what Italy has without being too far from what you're comfortable with. It's a university town with a lively nightlife mostly in the historical centre, and the surrounding countryside is gorgeous.' In 2000, she married Graham and the couple decided to look for a home of their own.

'We really wanted a garden but, although Bologna has beautiful apartments in and around the centre, houses with gardens are few and far between.' After a year, they found the property, which they eventually bought, in a magazine. In a tiny hamlet at the foot of the Apennines, it was newly built into the side of a hill on the site of a previous building. 'It consisted of four walls, a screed floor and a roof – no windows or doors, plaster, wiring or plumbing. But it had great potential and wonderful views.' However, an offer had already been accepted, although no money had changed hands yet. Graham and the estate agent leaned hard on the builder/owner to accept their cash deposit immediately and the sale subsequently went through in a couple of months.

Sonia Coady and her husband, Graham Ditchfield, took over a year to find the property they felt was right for them.

The question remained of how to get the house finished. Having received an astronomical quote from one company, Graham took their proposal, blanked out the fees and approached various firms for estimates on individual jobs. Picking the best price for each, he was able to get the work done within their budget. 'By taking on different firms you effectively take on the management of the entire project. It is guaranteed to generate stress and the way to combat it is to be patient and to take satisfaction as each day brings another addition, no matter how small. A whole new language of tools and building terms emerged as we battled linguistically with Neapolitan plasterers, Sicilian electricians, Bolognese diggers and Ferrarese builders, bringing Italian gesticulation to new heights!' A sturdy mountain house, it had two rooms on each of its three floors, with a staircase going up the centre. The garage and cellar have become a TV room, study and bathroom. The first floor comprises a large kitchen and living room, with two bedrooms and a bathroom upstairs. 'We wanted to be in by Christmas 2001 but the weather went against us. The builders couldn't get their truck up through the snow three times. Then we began to discover the things you can and can't do.' The heat efficiency engineer sent by the local council told them they needed special plaster and a film on all the windows to retain the heat. He also dictated the positions of the radiators. 'You do need a document from him for when you sell the property, but afterwards we discovered that some people get them falsified.' The council also insists that the extractor chimney is three metres higher than the apex of the roof 'which looks ridiculous', that a bathroom window must be one eighth the size of the bathroom itself (i.e. an eight-square-metre bathroom needs a one-square-metre window), and an outdoor barbecue must comply with planning permission. 'We kept discovering these things as we submitted the planning changes. People do take risks and ignore them – we know a couple of lovely houses that are still on the council documents as tool sheds – but you have to pay a hefty fine if found out.' Having at last completed the house and moved in, the next task they face is taming the 9,000 square metres of garden.

For nine months, building their home became 'an all-consuming, full-time task with nowhere to hide'.

Ex-pats

Lake Como
Wanda and Graham Nash

A return to her family's roots and a desire to learn more about the country led headmistress Wanda Nash and her husband Graham, a ship broker, to look for a second home in Italy. 'We decided we wanted to be somewhere within an hour's drive of Milan because of the easy, cheap flights from the UK, and thought the Lakes offered the best of both worlds – snow and skiing in the winter and water in the summer.' They wrestled with the choice of lakes, but plumped for Lake Como, only forty minutes north of Milan, not over developed and utterly beautiful. ' I always go back convinced it won't be as beautiful as I remember, but it always is. The lake is inky blue, the mountains tipped with snow and flowers everywhere.'

The Nashes contacted Casa Travella, a UK agency specializing in Italian property, who arranged for them to see various houses in the area over the next half-term break. 'At that point all we wanted was a studio or a one-bedroom flat. What we saw seduced us into looking for something much bigger, so friends and family could visit.' They worried that the areas surrounding houses overlooking the lake would be too busy in the summer and too quiet in the winter, and so they chose to go further into the mountains, where they could live in the heart of an Italian community.

Down a narrow, cobbled street in a small village they found a house that had been empty since 1940. It had two cellars built into the mountainside, a big, farmhouse kitchen and living room on the floor above, and two bedrooms at the top. The place was filled with wine-making equipment and wine bottles. 'It was very basic, with no heating or plumbing, but the rooms were a lovely size. It had a courtyard, a garden up the hillside and views of the mountains.' They knew it would take work, but its character and location were unbeatable. For £33,000, it was theirs. The agent was able to recommend a *geometra* (surveyor/architect) who told them that the structure was sound, but that the interior would have to be gutted. 'We thought we'd only have to install heating and do some decoration, but we ended up having new ceilings and floors throughout. That was a blow.' The estimate for the work came in at £35,000. By then they trusted their *geometra* and, at Christmas 2001, three months after they first saw it, the papers were

A forty-minute drive from Milan, Lake Como has not been over-developed and offers both winter and summer attractions.

signed and he began work. By February, the house was like an open barn with a view from the basement straight through to the roof. 'When we showed people photos, they were all doom and gloom but everything went even smoother than we'd envisaged.'

Although anxious to keep the character of the house, the Nashes had to compromise in having new beams, new tiles that looked old, and new, sealed wooden windows. However, they were able to keep the original doors and huge locks, and also the original open fireplace, which they took out during the building work and put back in later. Central heating, a new boiler and plumbing, new ceilings, floors and state-of-the-art bathrooms were all installed and the basement was converted into a utility room and storage area. By July, they had moved in. 'We keep pinching ourselves. We had an excellent team who went to incredible trouble over the details, lining the cupboards, adding shelves in the right wood, and more. It's much better than we'd ever imagined.'

They have been welcomed into the community who appreciated Wanda's Italian connections and fluent Italian. 'Everyone seems to know everything about us. When we had to have a wardrobe lifted in through an upstairs window, they were all out looking to see what

Above: The Nashes have restored their house from top to bottom, keeping it as true to its original character as possible.
Right: A fireplace, before and after.

was going on.' It was a stroke of luck that the *geometra*'s father-in-law lives next door but one. He keeps an eye on the property when they are away and turns the heating on for them in the winter. As for the idea of renting it while they are back at work in London: 'It's not for rent. It's so lovely, I couldn't bear the idea of sharing it.'

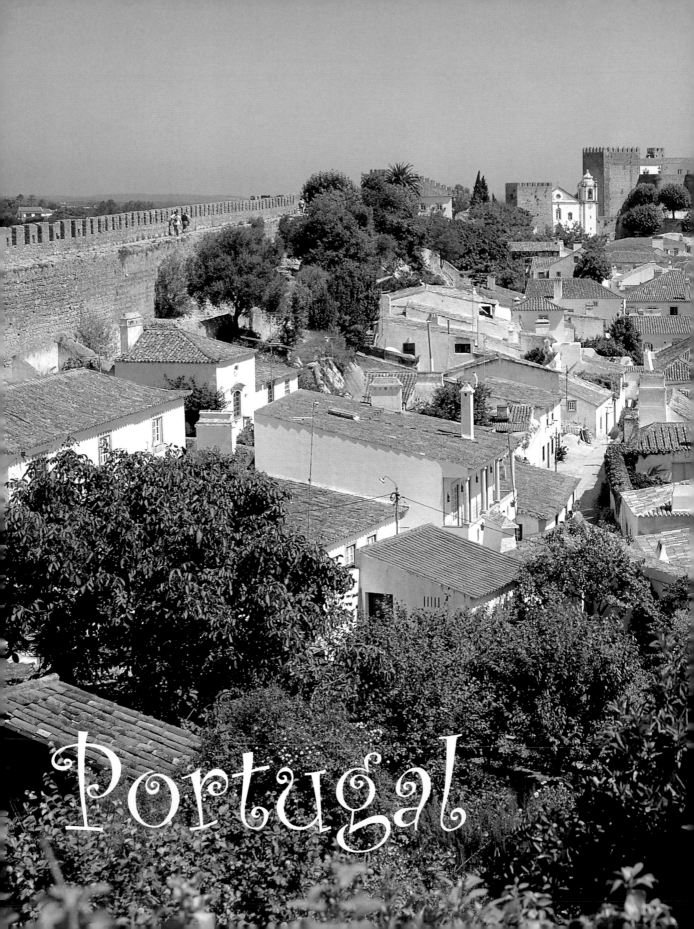

Portugal

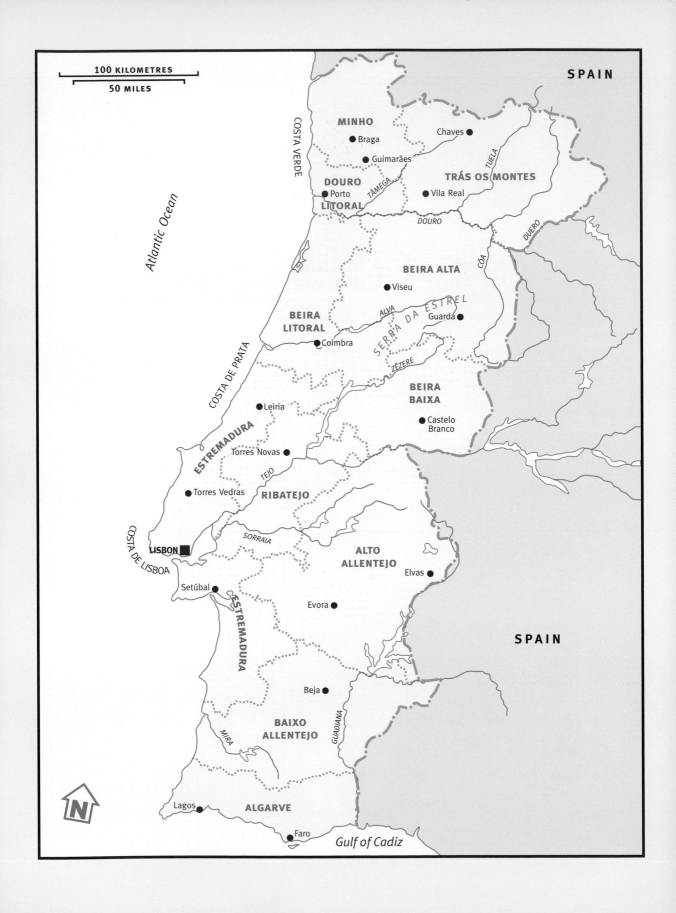

Portugal

Portugal holds a particular attraction for the British, a fact which can perhaps be explained by the strong ties formed through various historical treaties between the two countries. Indeed, Portugal can be considered to be one of Britain's oldest allies. Today, holidaymakers and home buyers flock to the pleasures offered by the Algarve coast and the area around Lisbon in particular, to cultural attractions that include Unesco World Heritage sites, among them Evora, Alcobaça and Sintra Vila, and to the unspoilt beauty of the many different landscapes – white beaches, undulating hills, rugged mountain ranges and the vast, fertile plain of the Alentejo.

Yet, the Portuguese nation has a long and stubborn history of independence, encouraged by its geography, bordered as it is on one side by the Atlantic and on the other by the mountains and rivers that divide it from Spain. In ancient Portuguese history, the Celtic and Roman civilizations loomed large. In the south, however, the pronounced Moorish influence is evident in the architecture and in the tradition of *azulejos*: bright, ceramic tiles that decorate even the most modest buildings.

After a long, seedy decline from its days as a great colonial power in South America and southern Africa, Portugal announced its modernization by rejecting the dictatorship of Salazar in 1970, embracing democracy, and joining the EU in 1986. Among many other economic and social improvements that came along with their membership, came funds for the expansion of motorways and the mechanization of farming. However, as befits an ancient and proud nation, time-honoured ways of life still persist in Portugal. Inland medieval villages remain relatively undeveloped, unchanged local markets sell local produce, calendar-festivals are held throughout the year, and traditions of craftsmanship are still in evidence everywhere. Most importantly, and most attractive of all, however, is the warm and generous spirit of the Portuguese people.

regions

Portugal presents many faces to the world. The Algarve coastline is renowned for its consistently excellent weather, smart resorts, designer villas, pristine beaches and international-standard golf courses. It has been a popular tourist resort for decades, and British people have flocked there both for holidays and to buy second homes. Further north lie the rolling agricultural plains of the Alentejo, with its historic, fortified villages, 'marble towns' and quieter, coastal resorts. Portugal's capital, Lisbon, has grown into a cosmopolitan city with a lively Moorish quarter which contrasts with the modern developments that sprang up when the city was chosen for Expo '98. Lisbon's surrounding coastline offers many attractions, including the elegant resorts of Cascais and Estoril and the historic towns of Sintra, Peniche and Obidos. Further north, Oporto is the principal town in an area mostly devoted to industry, business and, of course, Port wine. This prosperous region is dominated by the Douro river, with a coastline offering beaches, spas and a coastal pine forest. Yet, drive a few miles from

facts

CAPITAL: Lisbon
AREA: 92,391 sq km
COASTLINE: 1,793 km
POPULATION: 10,066,000
CURRENCY: Euro
TIME ZONE: GMT
ELECTRICITY: 220 volts
WEIGHTS AND MEASURES: metric
RELIGION: predominantly Roman Catholic
LANGUAGE: Portuguese
GOVERNMENT: parliamentary democracy
INTERNATIONAL DIALLING CODE: 00 351
INDEPENDENCE: 1140
NATIONAL HOLIDAY: Portugal Day, 10 June

the coast and you enter a rural landscape where life goes on much as it has for several centuries. Further inland still, the landscape is barren and mountainous.

Portugal is made up of eleven provinces. It is worth noting that the tourist board has redefined them into six regions: Costa Verde (the Green Coast in the north), Costa de Prata (the Silver Coast), Costa de Lisboa, the Algarve, Montanhas (the northern, mountainous region) and Planícies (the inland plains towards the south).

Algarve

DISTRICT: Faro
LANDSCAPE: golden sands with a rockier coastline to the west, further inland, green and undulating, with miles of citrus orchards, and almond and olive groves, rising to the mountainous Serra de Monchique, Serra do Caldeirão and Serra do Espinhaço de Cão
MAJOR TOWNS: Faro (capital), Lagos, Portimão, Loulé, Tavira, Silves, Sagres, Albufeira
HIGHLIGHTS: Parque Natural da Ria Formosa, Igreja da Misericórdia (Tavira), Castelo (Silves), Igreja de Santo António (Lagos), Fortaleza de Sagres
FESTIVALS: *Loulé Carnival* (February/March), *Prócession de Nossa Senhora da Piedade* (Loulé, May), *Festa e Feria de Senhora de Carmo* (Faro, July), *Festa de Senhora dos Mártires* (Castro Marim, August), Algarve Folk Music and Dance Festival (September), *Feria de Santa Iria* (Faro, October), Monchique Fair (October), *Festival do Morisco* (Olhão, August), *Festa da Cidade* (Tavira, June)
FOOD: *cataplana* (seafood stews), chicken piri-piri, oregano snails, roasted octopus, clams, fig pastries
DRINK: red wines of Lagoa, Lagos, Portimão and Tavira; liqueurs – Medronho, Brandymel
HANDICRAFTS: matgrass rugs, hand-painted ceramics, beaten copperware, lace
AIRPORT: Faro

Alto Alentejo

DISTRICTS: Evora, Portalegre
LANDSCAPE: wide open plains broken into huge agricultural estates, dotted with whitewashed towns and villages
MAJOR TOWNS: Évora, Portalegre Montemo-o-Novo, Ponte do Sor, Estremoz
HIGHLIGHTS: Évora, villages of Monsaraz and Marvão, dolmens and menhirs, Igreja de Nossa Senhora da Consolação, Parque Natural da Serra e São Mamede
FESTIVALS: *Festas do Senhor da Piedade e de São Mateus* (Elvas, September), *Feria de São João Évora* (June/July), *Festa de Nossa Senhora dos Passos* (Monsaraz, September)
HANDICRAFTS: tapestries (Portalegre), hand-painted furniture, woollen blankets and rugs, unglazed red pottery, embroidery (Nisa)
FOOD: *migus à alentejana* (bread stew), goat's and sheep's cheese from Évora, local sausages
DRINK: wines from Borba, Reguengos and Redondo

Baixo Alentejo

DISTRICT: Beja
LANDSCAPE: from rolling fields of wheat, cork and olive groves to the wind-blown, rugged Atlantic coast
MAJOR TOWNS: Beja, Moura Alcácer do Sal,

Along the coast of the Algarve, there are fishing villages such as Carvoeiro, which have remained unspoilt despite the influx of tourism.

Santiago do Cacém, Odemira, Vila Nova de Milfontes

HIGHLIGHTS: Parque Natural do Vale do Guadiana, Mértola, Convento da Conceição (Beja), Santa Clara dam

FESTIVAL: Ovibeja sheep fair (Beja, March)

HANDICRAFTS: arriolos rugs, ceramics, copper goods, lace

FOOD: *ensopada de borrego* (lamb stew), wild boar, *carne de porco à Alentejana* (pork stew), *ensopada de cabrito* (kid stew), *favada de caça* (rabbit or game with beans) goat's and sheep's cheese from Serpa

DRINK: some good small producers of local red wine

Beira Alta

DISTRICTS: Guarda and Viseu

LANDSCAPE: from mountainous ranges of the Serra da Estrela to wooded valleys of Douro in the south

MAJOR TOWNS: Viseu, Guarda

HIGHLIGHTS: Viseu cathedral, Museum of Grão Vasco (Viseu), Roman archaeological remains, Parque Natural da Serra da Estrela, spa springs (Caldas da Manteigas)

FESTIVALS: *Feria de São Mateus* (August/September), *Festa do Sortelha* (August), *Ciclo de Jazz* (Guarda, April)

HANDICRAFTS: black pottery, lace, basketry, woollen goods

FOOD: mountain cheeses, corn and rye breads, mountain kid, smoked hams

DRINK: red and white Dão wines; sparkling wines of the Lafões region

Beira Baixa

DISTRICT: Castelo Branco

LANDSCAPE: hilly in the north, with parched, open spaces in south

MAJOR TOWN: Castelo Branco

HIGHLIGHTS: fortified village of Monsanto, Palácio Episcopal (Castelo Branco), Roman remains at Idanha-a-Velha

FESTIVAL: *Festa das Cruzes* (Monsanto, May)

HANDICRAFTS: bedspreads (Castelo Branco)

FOOD: sheep's cheese

DRINK: Aguardiente

Beira Litoral

DISTRICTS: Coimbra, Aveiro

LANDSCAPE: lower part of the Costa de Prata (Silver Coast) with marshy wetlands inland to hillier landscape

MAJOR TOWNS: Coimbra, Leira, Aveiro, Figueira da Foz

HIGHLIGHTS: Coimbra, Conimbriga's Roman ruins, Buçaco National Forest, hilltop castle of Montemor-o-Velho

FESTIVALS: Burning of the Ribbons Festival (Coimbra, May), *Festa da Rainha Santa* (Coimbra, July), International Festival of Magic (Coimbra, September), *Festas da Cidade* (Figueras, June), *Festa de Março* (Aveiro, March)

HANDICRAFTS: porcelain (Vista Alegre), ceramics (Coimbra), decorative earthenware (Caldas da Rainha), glass and crystal (Alcobaça)

FOOD: fresh fish and shellfish, roast suckling pig, eel caldeirado, regional patries

DRINK: red and white wines from Buçaco

Above right: Away from the busy coastline, Portugal features rolling plains and isolated villages where life continues much as it has for centuries.
Below: A sizable expatriate community lives in Oporto, enjoying its proximity both to the sea and the Douro valley.

Douro Litoral

DISTRICT: Porto
LANDSCAPE: the southern part of the Costa Verde backed by pine forest, cut across by the Douro river estuary
MAJOR TOWN: Oporto
HIGHLIGHTS: Oporto's old Ribeira district, Contemporary Art Museum (Oporto), Igreja de Nossa Senhora dos Remédios (Lamego)
FESTIVALS: *Festa do São Gonçalo* (Amarante, June), *Festa de São João* (Oporto, June)
HANDICRAFTS: lace and woollen goods
FOOD: tripe, seafood – especially cod, smoked hams, Amarante pastries
DRINK: wines – port, vinho verde, sparkling wine of Lamego
AIRPORT: Oporto

Estremadura

DISTRICTS: Leiria, Evora, Setúbal
LANDSCAPE: narrow coastal strip, with pine forest west of Leiria
MAJOR TOWNS: Lisbon, Setúbal, Cascais, Estoril, Sesimbra
HIGHLIGHTS: Lisbon's historic and cultural treasures, monasteries at Batalha and Alcobaça, palaces at Mafra, Queluz, Sintra, medieval village of Óbidos, caves at Mira de Aire, Fátima (Pilgrim's walk, May)
FESTIVALS: numerous festivals in Lisbon, Cascais, Estoril, *Festas do Colete Encarnado* (Vila Franco de Xira, July), Estoril Handicrafts Fair (July/August), *Festa do Santiago* (Setúbal, July/August), Sea Festival (Sesimbra, September), pilgrimage of Nossa Senhora da Nazaré (Sitío, September)
HANDICRAFTS: lace, pottery, basketwork, quilts
FOOD: seafood including Portuguese oysters and sardines, goat's and sheep's cheese, local pastries, orange marmelade, Belem's *pastais de nata* (pastries)
DRINK: red wines from Colares; white wines from Bucelas; reds and whites from Setúbal;

Manteigas is one of the most attractive towns in the Parque Natural da Serra da Estrela. Close to the spa centre of Caldas de Manteigas, it also provides an excellent base for exploring the area.

The fortified hill-top town of Monsaraz enjoys an unparalleled view across the Alentejo.

HANDICRAFTS: lace, Barcelos pottery, linen, cutlery, gold and silverware, embroidery, shoes
FOOD: fish – including *lampreia* (eel), *salmão* (salmon) and *bacalhau* (dried cod), *rojões* (pork and sausage), *caldo verde* (cabbage, potato and sausage soup)
DRINK: *vinho verde* (white wine)

Ribatejo

DISTRICT: Santarém
LANDSCAPE: fertile river valley with pastures, wheat fields, fig, citrus and olive groves
MAJOR TOWN: Santarém
HIGHLIGHTS: Convento de Cristo (Tomar), Castelo de Almourol
FESTIVALS: *Festival Nacional de Gastronómia* (Santarém, October), *Festa dos Tabuleiros* (Festival of the Trays, Tomar, every four years, July), *Procession of Nossa Senhora da Piedade* (Tomar, every second September)
HANDICRAFTS: rush baskets, patchwork quilts, glazed and hand-painted pottery
FOOD: rice, vegetables, goat's cheese, shad, *sopa da pedra* (stone soup)
DRINK: red wines from Cartaxo; white wines from Chamusca, Alpiarça and Almeirim

Tras-os-Montes

DISTRICTS: Bragança, Vila Real
LANDSCAPE: hostile mountain terrain with fertile Douro valley further south
MAJOR TOWNS: Bragança, Vila Real, Chaves, Miranda do Douro
HIGHLIGHTS: Roman bridge at Chaves, medieval city of Bragança, Museu de Abade de Baçal (Bragança), Barragem de Miranda, Parque Natural de Montesinho, thermal springs
FESTIVALS: *Feria de Todos Santos* (Chaves, October/November), *Dia de Cidade* (Chaves, July), *Feira das Canarinha* (Bragança, May)
HANDICRAFTS: weaving, earthenware
FOOD: smoked ham, sausages, local pastries
DRINK: *vinho verde*, Mateus Rosé, red and sparkling whites of São Neutel, reds of Vespasiano, reds and white of Flavius

dessert wine – Moscatel (Sesimbra)
AIRPORT: Lisbon

Minho

DISTRICTS: Braga, Viana do Castelo
LANDSCAPE: a wild, unspoilt coastline with wooded hills, lush valleys and vineyards further inland
MAJOR TOWNS: Braga, Guimaraes, Viana do Castelo
HIGHLIGHTS: Parc Nacional da Peneda-Gerês, Braga Cathedral, remains of Celtic hill settlement at Citânia de Briteiros, fortress of Valença do Minho, Roman bridge at Ponte de Lima
FESTIVALS: Easter week (Braga), *Festas de São João* (Braga, June), *Festas das Cruzes* (Barcelos, May), *Romaria de Nossa Senhora da Agonia* (Viana do Castelo, August), *Feiras Novas* (Ponte de Barca, August)

Property

By far the majority of the estimated 100,000 Britons owning property in Portugal have opted for the pleasures of the Algarve with the result that, in some areas, prices have as much as doubled in the last three years. The Algarve's British community is well served by the Four Seasons country club, various time-share clubs, fitness, bridge and bowls clubs with British bars and restaurants thrown in. The *Algarve Resident* is a weekly publication (in newsagents and on the Net) containing information about events and exchange and property columns.

British buyers tend to spread throughout the region, but are particularly concentrated between Lagos and São Brás de Alportal. The most expensive locations are along the coast, most particularly in the central area known as the 'Golden Triangle', which includes Vale do Lobo, Quinta do Lago and Loulé. As a result of the overflow from the Golden Triangle, other areas are being developed, such as the region around Vilamoura, and east of Faro towards Tavira and the Spanish border. Prices here tend to be a little lower than in the centre. Modern complexes nearer the coast are extremely popular. These can feature splendid, two to five-bedroom, detached villas of varying designs surrounded by their own land, less spacious two to three-bedroom

Once a tiny fishing village, Cascais has become one of the most popular coastal resorts near Lisbon, where traditional Portuguese homes rub shoulders with sophisticated modern apartment blocks.

The Algarve is famous for its immaculate championship-level golf courses.

terraced houses, or apartments of varying sizes which have the use of communal gardens and a pool. Most complexes are built near golf courses, and some offer a vast range of facilities from spas, gyms and hairdressers, to restaurants, bars and tennis courts. Before buying, it is wise to check if there are any annual condominium charges and, if there are, what exactly they cover. For instance, golf club membership and green fees are often charged extra, albeit with a discount if you own property in the complex. Cheaper complexes will have fewer or no facilities, relying on their proximity to a nearby town or village. If buying off-plan, make sure you know exactly where your property will be situated, what other building plans exist for the area around it and which fixtures, fittings and details are included in the price.

Traditional homes can still be found in fishing villages along the coast which retain their old-world charm. However, some home owners prefer to escape inland to the hills where their Euros stretch further and where they can enjoy the 'real' Portugal. Moorish influences can still be seen in the low, whitewashed houses, which have pointed, four-sided, tiled or terraced roofs. Most distinctive of all are the chimneys: tall, slender and intricately filigreed with a crowning ornament of some kind, and the hand-painted glazed tiles, found on both inside walls and out. Larger farmhouses, estate or manor houses (*quintas*) can still be found for restoration (though they are becoming hard to come by), usually with thick stone walls, small or no windows (to protect against extremes of temperature) and two or three bedrooms. Often too dilapidated to renovate, it is easier to demolish and start again, salvaging original features such as walls, fireplaces, doors or windows. Gaining planning permission is unlikely to be a problem if you are building on the footprint of an existing building, although there will be limitations on how far it can be extended, depending on the size of the plot and the region in which it is located. Similarly, if you are building from scratch, there are likely to be limitations on the square meterage and height of any proposed building. Dealing with the *cámera* (local authorities) can involve nightmarish bureaucracy (financial backhanders have been known to oil the wheels) and changes of heart, so make sure planning permission is granted before buying the property. The government is keen to prevent too much modern building, and it is unlikely that you will be able to depart far from the Portuguese traditional style. In most areas, there aren't any grants available to help with restoration.

The area around Lisbon is another hot spot for foreigners buying their own piece of the sun, although the market has slowed down over the last few years. Few buy in the city itself, where property is generally expensive and largely limited to apartments, often with additional service charges to cover the maintenance of the common parts. The most popular properties are those in the Alfama district, in the Pombalino-style buildings in the centre with their typical *janelas verdes* (green shutters) and in the Lapa district, largely home to ambassadors and businessmen. However, Cascais, Estoril and Sintra, the three main resorts on the Costa de Lisboa, offer plenty of opportunities to buy into villa or apartment complexes, although prices have risen sharply in recent years. Older buildings tend to be simply built out of local limestone, and are often decorated with stucco and cornicing.

There's a long history of British people living and trading in Oporto. As a result, there's a strong British community with established lawn tennis and cricket clubs, a British school and Protestant church. The most popular area is Oporto's 'mini-Riviera' of Foz a few miles north of the city where, along with other coastal or

Lisbon's Alfama is the old Moorish quarter whose houses, adorned with wrought iron balconies, still retain their authentic character.

riverside locations, property is at its most expensive. Two to four-bedroom town houses are popular, mostly coming with verandas, terraces or gardens, the latter adding to the price. Predictably, houses in the country are larger and cheaper in the *quinta* style, although along the Douro valley unadorned cottages rub shoulders with *solares* (grand manor houses) on the old country estates. As elsewhere, planning permission is not always easy to obtain, the criteria for passing plans often remaining unclear.

Further North is the Minho, an area growing in popularity with British home-buyers who are particularly concentrated in Afife, Viano do Castelo and Porde do Limo, though many have bought inland too, where old houses have been left by local Portuguese people who have relocated to the cities for work. Renovated, these houses are expensive, but there are ruined *quintas* to be found that typically offer both privacy and land. Usually built of granite, they have tiled roofs and small chimneys or just gaps to let the smoke out. The *cámera* adheres to the stricture that old properties must be rebuilt in the same style as the original, retaining whatever original features remain. Ideally, pictures should be provided of the house, past and present, before the town hall's architects visit the property to agree planning stipulations.

Prices are rising in the more popular areas of Portugal but if you search further afield, real bargains can still be found. However, remote regions are still poorly serviced by road and rail, and housing can be still fairly primitive. The foreigners buying in Tras-os-Montes, for example, are rare. Here, shale and slate are the dominant materials and housing is primitive, conditions are harsh and communications undeveloped, discouraging anyone but the most intrepid loners. In the Alentejo, whitewashed houses are mostly one-storeyed with yellow or blue skirtings, with small windows and doors. They tend to be dominated by the huge, domed chimneys needed for the fires in the freezing winters – an attractive, practical style. Many foreign buyers are put off by the weather, but some buy in this region for its guaranteed peace and tranquillity.

You may not feel daunted by the amount of work required to bring a property up to the standard you require, but you may find that the labour is harder to find and of less good quality than in the busier areas, where the service infrastructure has been better developed. Busier areas also have the obvious advantage that schools, shops and medical facilities are more easily accessible, a fact worth keeping in mind when choosing an area in which to live.

how to find property in Portugal

Having settled on the area in which you want to live, scour the international property magazines, national newspapers and the Net for properties for sale. Visit the international property exhibitions that feature homes in Portugal. They are usually advertised in local and national newspapers, and take place regularly throughout the UK. If in Portugal itself, check the local papers and expatriate magazines such as *Algarve Property Advertiser*, the *Portugal Post* or *The Anglo-Portuguese News*. Lists of agents can also be obtained from the UK Portuguese Chamber of Commerce, the Association of Portuguese Estate Agents (APEMI), or the Federation of Overseas Property Developers Agents and Consultants (FOPDAC). If dealing directly with a Portuguese estate agent whom you may have found via the Net, local newspapers or just by scouting out the area, make sure they are government-licenced (*mediador autorizado*). A good Portuguese agent can handle the whole purchase for you from the moment you view the property, right down to arranging connection to mains services. Strictly speaking, there is no need to employ a solicitor unless you are in any way uncertain of how things are progressing, although, unless you are versed in the language, you may sleep more easily at night knowing a legal expert, familiar with the laws and tax systems of both countries, is supervising your affairs.

Traditional features of a Portuguese house can include elaborately carved doors, painted door and window reliefs and a balcony on the roof terrace.

How to buy a property in Portugal

All would-be property buyers must obtain a fiscal tax card (*cartão de contribuinte*) available from the local tax office on production of a passport and Portuguese address. With it comes a fiscal number, essential in all future dealings with the tax authorities or local *notario* and when it comes to registering the title deed of your property with the land registry.

Before you buy a property in Portugal, your lawyer should confirm with the land registry office, *Conservatório do Registo Predial*, that it is registered in the vendor's name and is free of any debts or mortgages. If the property is owned by various members of a family, each one must have agreed to the sale. You will not be pleased when a distant relative appears claiming his share after you believed the deal was sealed. At this stage, you should consider in whose name it is best for the property to be registered. This will have implications on the inheritance tax payable by your heirs.

The process of buying property in Portugal is well-regulated and can be conducted by the estate agent, but it is subject to change, and so it is advisable to have a lawyer (*advogado* or *solicitador*) to check the procedure for you. Either use a British-based solicitor specialising in Portuguese property law or a local solicitor who may be recommended by your estate agent or, far better, by someone who has employed him or her before.

Generally, there are two stages to go through. The preliminary contract (*contrato promesso de compra e venda*) is binding to the buyer and seller and is drawn up by the seller's representative. It contains a description of the property, confirmation of the identities of both buyer and seller, confirmation of the completion date, confirmation of the 'clear title' of ownership, any conditional clauses and the deposit agreement. Before signing, the seller should produce all the relevant paperwork for your solicitor to check, including a habitation licence (*licence de habitação*) if the property was built after 1951, and the tax document (*caderneta predial urbana*). The latter will contain a description of the property that should be checked against the title deed, the name under which it is registered, the date it was registered and its official value. A deposit of 10 per cent of the purchase price is payable by the buyer on signature of this agreement. If the buyer subsequently withdraws then this amount is forfeited, whereas if the seller withdraws he will be liable to pay double the deposit.

The resort of Vilamoura offers championship golf courses, holiday villages with investment opportunities for home buyers, a casino and a vast marina.

Above: Once occupied by warehouses, Lisbon's dock area is now a fashionable residential district alive with plenty of restaurants and bars.
Right: The white-washed walls and terracotta roofs of the houses characterize the fortified medieval town of Obidos.

At this stage, the buyer must import the necessary funds to pay for the property, plus extra related costs such as legal fees (about 2 per cent of purchase price), and notary and land registry fees (about 1 per cent). Property transfer tax (SISA) could be anything up to 10 per cent depending on the declared value of the property, and is paid at the local tax office. If the property is already in the name of an offshore company, the buyer will be exempt from paying SISA. However, the Portuguese government have recently introduced a higher rate of local rates and taxes for offshore registered properties. Seek advice before buying a property in this way.

The second stage of the purchase is the conveyance (*escritura*) that is signed by both the buyer and seller (or by whomever they have granted power of attorney to conduct their affairs) in the presence of a notary *(notario)* after he has read the contract aloud to them both. If you cannot speak Portuguese, you must have a translator present. The notary will want to see copies of the seller's habitation licence, the SISA receipt, the fiscal numbers and passports for buyers (or their power of attorney). The balance of the money due must be passed over at this stage and the property will be transferred into the name of the buyer.

There are two other procedures for which the buyer is responsible. He or she must arrange registration with the Land Registry (*Conservatória*) by submitting a copy of the *escritura* to provide conclusive proof of ownership and with the Inland Revenue (*Repartição de Finanças*) for eventual payment of rates and taxes on the property.

mortgages

You may be fortunate enough to have sufficient funds for a cash purchase. If not, you may be able to raise some or all the finance necessary for your purchase by re-mortgaging your home in the UK. Many home buyers decide to secure a loan against the Portuguese property with a Portuguese bank, or a branch of a foreign bank or building society operating in the country. Generally, a mortgage of up to 75 per cent, to be repaid over 15 years can be obtained. Remember to take into account the arrangement fees when you are budgeting for your purchase. These can amount to 4 per cent of the amount borrowed. Shop around until you are sure you are getting the best value you can. Buying through an offshore company is a popular way of buying property in Portugal. It means the buyer does not pay inheritance tax or capital gains tax when they resell their property. There are many serious drawbacks to owning via a company.

insurance

On mortgaged property, the bank will usually make sure that you have valid buildings insurance and valid life assurance to cover the outstanding mortgage balance on all persons to whom the mortgage was granted. Otherwise, it is advisable to take out a

good insurance policy covering third-person liability, theft and damage. Shop around for the best policy and read the small print to check, among other things, that the property is covered if it stands empty over a certain period of time.

inheritance law

The most notable features of traditional Algarve houses are their chimneys – tall, slender and topped with intricate latticework and ornament.

Like other European countries, Portugal does have an inheritance law which dictates that an estate be split compulsorily to give each of the deceased's children a fixed share. However, unless a foreigner dies without making a will, it does not generally apply to foreigners who may make a will according to the laws of their own country. An English will is valid in Portugal but it may take months for probate to be granted. It is better to make a separate Portuguese will covering your Portuguese property. This can be one of two kinds. The more common of the two is a public will, which is entered into the notarial books as if it were a deed. Written in Portuguese, it is signed in front of the notary and two witnesses. If you cannot speak Portuguese, you must have a translator present. The second option is a private will. This can be written in English, although you will also have to provide a Portuguese translation of it. It must be signed in front of two witnesses and the notary who will seal it and return it to you, although you may ask him to look after it.

The old fishing village of Albufeira has become one of the Algarve's busiest resorts, where tourists are drawn by the huge beaches and buzz of restaurants, bars and clubs.

Living in Portugal

residency

All EU nationals are entitled to visit Portugal for 90 days at a time, though they should register their presence with their Embassy after fourteen days. This is almost never done. If proposing to move there permanently, a residence card (*autorização de residência*) is required. This can be obtained from the Foreigners' Department (*Serviço de Estrangeiros e Fronteiras*) of the Portuguese Ministry of Foreign Affairs, which has offices in most of the larger cities. If unemployed and wanting permanent residency, you must provide proof that you can support yourself financially, or that someone else can. Retirees to Portugal can stay for 180 days, officially extending their visitor status after 90 days before applying for their full *autorização de residência*.

work

If proposing to move permanently to Portugal and work for a living, do not underestimate the difficulties of obtaining a job, unless you have arranged something before moving. Your Portuguese will need to be fluent to convince a potential employer

furniture and goods

If establishing a permanent residence in Portugal, you can transport any furniture and goods into the country free of customs duties provided that you have owned them for six months or more. Be warned, there is a fair amount of bureaucratic form-filling to be done.

government

Portugal is a republic headed by a President, who is elected for a maximum of two consecutive five-year terms. The Prime Minister represents the parliamentary majority and is appointed by the President. The legislative authority, the single chambered *Assembleía da República*, is elected every four years by popular vote. The President also appoints a Minister of the Republic for all of the autonomous regions who in turn appoints a regional Government President. Mainland Portugal is divided into eighteen *distritos* (districts) which subdivide into *concelhos* (boroughs), each with a *paço do concelho* (town hall) and a *cámera municipal* (executive committee) run by the mayor. Health, finance and education are dealt with at a district level. Finally, the *concelhos* are broken down into *freguesias* (parishes) responsible for maintaining local heritage, keeping public records and organising local events.

that you are a better bet than a Portuguese person competing for the same job. If planning to set up a business of your own, take care to investigate the detail thoroughly and provide for all the pitfalls that may occur. The bureaucracy involved will be complex and frustrating. An EU national does not need a work permit to work in another EU country.

social security

Portugal has a social security system (*Caixa de Previdência*) similar to the UK's, though contributions are relatively higher. The system covers employed and self-employed individuals while others can register voluntarily. Leaflet SA 29 from the DSS gives details of social security, pension rights and healthcare within the EU.

bank account

This will be necessary and convenient for payment of tax and utility bills. Find the bank that suits you best through personal recommendations, bearing in mind the convenience of its location and whether they speak English. You will need to present proof of identification, address and your fiscal number. Remember that in Portugal, a bounced cheque is considered fraudulent. Offshore banking in tax havens such as the Channel Islands or Gibraltar is another option, but be sure to check the credit rating of the bank you choose, the charges for starting up and running an account, and any restrictions they may impose on the withdrawal of funds. It would be wise to seek independent financial advice when considering the implications of this option.

The Portuguese have long relied on the sea for food, with fish, particularly cod, being one of the most important elements of their cuisine.

taxes

INCOME TAX: For tax purposes, an individual is resident in Portugal if they spend more than 183 days in Portugal in a year, or have what is considered a permanent home on 31 December of that year. A family is considered resident in Portugal if either spouse is a resident. Any resident is liable to Portuguese income tax on their worldwide income. It is a good idea to obtain independent financial advice on how judicious tax-planning may benefit you. Tax is assessed annually with returns due between February and May, the exact date depending on the type of income. Non-residents are taxed on their Portuguese income only. A double tax treaty exists between Portugal and the UK.

PROPERTY TAX: Property tax (*contribuição autáquica*) is paid annually in one or two instalments by property owners. The tax is based on the fiscal value of the house, which in turn is based by the government on the location, local services and market value of the property.

CAPITAL GAINS TAX: Capital gains tax (*imposto de mais*

Valias) is payable on any profit made on the sale of a house. It is based on the fiscal not the market value of the property. It is not payable if the property is owned by an offshore company (because the property is not sold, only the company), but other taxes may be due.

INHERITANCE TAX: Inheritance tax is paid by those inheriting assets from a Portuguese resident. Even if you are a non-resident, it is liable on inherited property in Portugal. The amount depends on the closeness of the inheritor's relationship with the deceased and the value of the inheritance. Inheritance tax is not liable if the property is owned through an offshore company.

VAT: The standard rate is 17 per cent, although plans to raise it to 19 per cent have just been announced.

mains services

ELECTRICITY: Electricity is provided by EDP (Electricidade de Portugal). Before you buy a property, make sure all its previous bills have been paid. Either you or your estate agent should register the new ownership with EDP, signing a contract giving your permanent address or that of your fiscal representative as security for payment of bills.

GAS: Gas is a rarity in Portugal. It is supplied by Gás de Portugal but only available in Lisbon. Otherwise, bottled or cylinder gas is used, easily available from local shops.

WATER: Contact your local town hall (*cámera municipal*) about supply details, making sure all previous bills have been paid before you buy your property. Register your permanent address or that of your fiscal representative. Costs vary from region to region but water is usually metered and paid for monthly. Some regions suffer from extreme water shortages during the hottest months. Outside towns and villages, mains water is harder to come by and even then, a continuous supply is not always guaranteed during the summer, so *cisternas* (private water tanks), wells and septic tanks may be needed.

education

If you are moving permanently to Portugal with your children, their education will be one of your prime concerns. If they are of secondary school age and you have decided against a UK boarding school in favour of immersing them in a new culture, then entering them in one of the fee-paying International or British schools is a good option. These operate in the major towns in areas most popular with ex-patriates: the Algarve, Lisbon and Oporto. Before choosing one, visit those in your area, checking they provide all they claim and choosing the one that will suit your child best and which offers your preferred educational system. Pre-school education in Portugal is optional and privately run when available. Between the ages of six and fifteen, a state system of education (*ensino básico*) operates that is compulsory and free, though parents are charged for books and stationery. It is divided into three stages that last for four, two and two years. If completed successfully, a certificate of basic education is awarded. Optional secondary education can be general (*cursos gerais*), vocational (*cursos tecnológicos*) or specialized artistic education (*cursos do ensino artístico especializado*). The resulting Secondary Education Diploma (*diploma de ensino segundo*) leads to further education at either university or polytechnic college. There are also private

cars

A foreign car can be imported provided it has been registered in the owner's name for over six months or has clocked up more than 6000 km. After compulsory re-registration in Portugal, it cannot be sold within the first year. All vehicles must have an annual check after the first four years. Non-residents can drive on a foreign licence for six months. EU residents can use their existing licence until it expires, but must then apply for a Portuguese licence.

pets

Provided your pets have an up-to-date Anti-Rabies Vaccination certificate, they will be allowed to enter Portugal without a quarantine period. They will not be allowed back into the UK without a pet passport.

schools operating in Portugal that are part funded by the state. Details can be obtained from the Portuguese Ministry of Education in Lisbon. Until recently, there has been a high level of illiteracy in Portugal, but the government has been working to improve the previously uneven standards of education and the curriculum. The immediate advantage of opting for the Portuguese education system is that it will enable a young child to pick up the language and be absorbed into the local community very quickly. Contact the nearest *cámera municipal* (town hall) for information on local schools.

healthcare

Portugal operates a free health service through its *centros de saúde* (health centres) and hospitals in every town. Residents are entitled to free medical care on presentation of a *cartão de utente* obtainable from a health

Above: Carvoeiro may have grown in popularity with foreign home owners over the years, but life in the harbour goes on unchanged. Below: The extraordinary sandstone formations of Ponta de Piedade lie just south of the busy town of Lagos.

centre. To get it, a resident must provide two photos, their ID card and proof of address. However, while treatment may be good, waiting lists can be long and hospitals overcrowded. Many opt for private treatment, in which case it is advisable to take out private insurance since charges tend to be high like anywhere else. There are numerous private clinics operating in the popular tourist areas, some of which are internationally run and use English doctors. It is possible to register with the doctor of your choice, Portuguese or otherwise, but remember to keep receipts to charge against tax. Private clinics advertise in the yellow pages and ex-patriate newspapers, but it is always sensible to ask around for recommendations. To qualify for any free treatment under the state system, you must be a resident paying social service contributions or a pensioner. Taking out additional private insurance would be advisable. For minor complaints, it is often preferable to ask advice at a local *farmácia* (chemist) where the qualified pharmacists can usually offer invaluable help.

If a non-resident, presentation of the E111 certificate (available from a UK post office) and passport entitles you to free emergency health treatment. The E111 is valid for two years. Make any claims for refunds as directed on the form. It is also wise to take out additional private insurance since you should expect to pay for any private medical treatment, medicines and dental treatment. An E106 form (from the DSS) gives British nationals reciprocal health cover for two years after a move abroad.

House hunters

Algarve
Richard Whiteley and Kathryn Apanowicz

The Algarve is Portugal's most popular stretch of coastline, renowned for its year-round sunshine, sandy beaches, fishing villages, and popular tourist resorts. Although it has a Mediterranean feel, it is washed by the Atlantic which prevents the summer heat from becoming too stifling. It occupies the southernmost part of Portugal, and its name derives from the Arabic, 'Al Gharb', meaning 'land to the west' or 'the land beyond.' Reclaimed from once inaccessible marshland, the region now boasts no fewer than ten national parks, twenty-seven golf courses and 150 glorious beaches. Of the ten million visitors that flock here every year, a quarter is made up of British holidaymakers coming to sample the

laid-back, friendly, family-centred atmosphere. Property is highly sought after, particularly within the area known as the Golden Triangle in central Algarve. In this area, a single plot can cost as much as three million pounds, making it one of the most expensive places to buy property in Europe. Elsewhere, however, traditional Portugal can still be found in unspoilt, coastal villages and quiet, inland towns.

TV presenter Richard Whiteley has been holidaying in the Algarve for the past twenty years with the result that he knows the area well and has plenty of friends there. He and his partner, radio and TV presenter Kathryn Apanowicz, decided to invest in their own holiday home, 'something quirky that people will remember', within a budget of £400,000.

VILAMOURA is one of the largest resorts in Portugal with its own marina, several beaches, restaurants, five-star hotels and the region's biggest disco. In the high season, the population swells to around 500,000. Its main attraction is the four, championship-level golf courses open all the year round. Overlooking one of them was a designer, four-bedroom villa, the winner of a 1998 International Design Award and on the market at £390,000. It successfully combined traditional décor with modern comforts. The open-plan living/dining room was vast, with an unusual, church-like quality, thanks to the stained-glass windows, floor and wall tiles. There was an appealing study with wall-to-wall wooden shelving, and the bedrooms were large and comfortable in idiosyncratic French and Hollywood styles. It also included four bathrooms, a sauna, a two-car garage, a

Above: This three-bedroom villa in the heart of Vilamoura combined contemporary comfort with traditional décor.
Below: Three acres of mature gardens surrounded a nineteenth-century quinto in need of renovation.

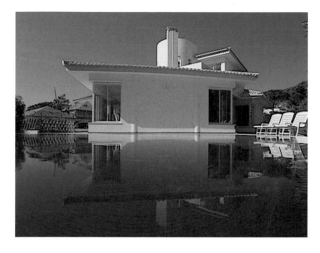

guest apartment and a pool. 'I was expecting the usual villa in the sun interior, but this was very Portuguese. But all the same, it's not right for us.'

Algarve's largest inland town is **LOULÉ**. It still fields evidence of the many invaders who have occupied it over the centuries, including the Phoenicians, Carthaginians, Romans and Moors. Today, it is known for its large market, selling everything from fresh fruit and vegetables to handicrafts. Although it is only a couple of miles from the Golden Triangle, property prices are noticeably lower. Here, Richard and Kathryn were able to view a nineteenth-century *quinta* (manor house) in need of renovation. The façade was hidden behind sprawling maple trees and inside were fifteen rooms, many of them currently used for storage, including four bathrooms and two kitchens, one with an original bread oven. Outside, there was a garage, two wells, a walled garden and three acres of matured grounds. Renovating this wonderful property would present a real challenge, but Richard was initially unphased. 'I like a challenge and this is certainly that. There would be a lot of work but it would be in a good cause.' A local builder estimated that all the structural work (to include knocking walls through to make larger rooms, repairing any cracks and installing a new kitchen and bathroom) would cost around £20,000. This kind of property is much in demand and, tempting as it was, Richard was realistic enough to see that it would be tremendously time-consuming, and that in fact it would be far too big for them.

So they went on to look in **QUINTA DO LAGO**, the most upmarket resort in the heart of the Golden Triangle, where prices can rise to twice those in the rest of Portugal. Less than 10 per cent of the land is developed, with buildings spread discreetly over its 2,000 acres. A popular haven for the rich and famous, it offers two miles of beach, four golf courses, a tennis academy, a health and fitness club, riding stables and water sports facilities. Most of the houses within the resort carry price tags of £750,000, but just outside was a luxury villa on the market for £402,000. Three bedrooms shared the ground floor with the living room and kitchen, while an elegant, spiral staircase led upstairs to the master-bedroom suite, complete with dressing room, shower room and jacuzzi. There was a roof terrace, a basement garage ready for conversion, a small garden and an environmentally friendly salt-water pool. 'It reminded me of a Malibu beach house – inside it was lovely, light and white with chic maple floors.' But there wasn't enough outdoor space for Richard and Kathryn, it was just over their budget, and, most importantly of all, they felt that the location was all wrong.

Finally, they went inland to the hills around the traditional Portuguese town of **SÃO BRAS DE ALPORTEL**. A friend had brought Richard there twenty years ago, when it was a simple, market town. Although it is more developed now and the surrounding hills are dotted with new villas, it has not lost any of its traditional charm and Richard sees it as his 'spiritual home'. Prices

Above: A luxury villa in the exclusive resort of Quinta do Lago. Below: A farmhouse lovingly restored with reclaimed materials retained many original features.

are about 25 per cent lower than on the coast, although they are beginning to rise as the area becomes more popular with home buyers on the hunt for the 'real' Portugal. A restored three-bedroom farmhouse nearby was on the market for £299,000. It had a striking atrium entrance, a large, light living room with an original bread oven, a dining room sporting the original fireplace and a modern, partly-fitted kitchen underneath the old chimney. Otherwise, there were two bathrooms, a wine cellar, a well-appointed guest house, a covered courtyard, a swimming pool and half an acre of garden with orange trees. 'I was thrilled when I first saw it. It met all the criteria I'd set myself. It's the right type of house, the right age and it has been so lovingly restored, using reclaimed wood and tiles.' The property had been on the market for eighteen months and the price had been recently reduced. Not wanting to rush into anything, Richard and Kathryn returned to the UK and ten days later asked a Portuguese friend to put in a bid on their behalf. Three days later, they received a telephone call to say it had already been sold. They were disappointed, but then, after friends had visited the property and encouraged them to buy it, Richard decided to fight back. Coincidentally, another friend happened to know the owner, who lived in London. 'I went to see him on a Thursday. He told me that the buyer was committed to raising the finances by midday on Friday. If that didn't happen, and it looked unlikely that it would, he would accept my offer of £280,000.' Richard drove back to Yorkshire sure he would be successful, but suddenly consumed by doubts as to whether he was doing the right thing. But on Friday afternoon he heard that the other buyer had come through after all – with an agreed sum less than the amount Richard had offered. On realizing he'd lost it, any second thoughts vanished and he was just tremendously disappointed. 'It seems that it was on the books of several estate agents, with none of them really knowing what the others were doing. Because it had been on the market for all that time, I didn't think I needed to hurry, but I've learned my lesson ready for next time: if you like something, act immediately.'

Above and below: A restored thee-bedroom farmhouse near São Bras de Alportel met all the criteria Richard Whiteley had set for a holiday home.

House hunters

Minho
Jim and Pat Mott

Minho is among the least spoilt regions of Portugal. Situated on the Costa Verde, on the border with Spain, it enjoys unpredictable weather but has blessedly short winters. The march of time has left the area almost untouched. Its three main towns, Braga, Viana do Castelo and Guimarães, are still provincial and surrounded by a lush landscape that leads to long stretches of undeveloped coastline. Minho boasts the only National Park in Portugal, Parc National da Peneda-Gerês, where the old hill farms and traditional ways of working the land still endure. The region is steeped in culture, with plenty of superbly restored historic houses, *festas* (costume festivals) and weekly markets. A new motorway has recently been opened through the heart of the region which, with the improved flight connections between the UK and Porto, means that the region is opening up to second-home buyers and attracting international property investment.

Retired sociology lecturer Jim Mott and his wife Pat sold their flat in the Algarve town of Tavira, and travelled north in search of the traditional, more historic Portugal. They were open-minded as to the type of property they were looking for, provided it had a garden and fell within their budget of £130,000. They began their search in the mountains near **REBORDOES**, an agricultural village where traditional farming methods are still practised. Local pine forests provide the wood for making barrels which contain Minho's most famous export, *Vinho Verde*. On the edge of the forest stood a one-storey, three-bedroom house which included a bathroom, a modern, tiled kitchen with chestnut fittings, a long, open living/dining room with a tiled floor,

A modernised three-bedroom house shaded by the pine woods near Rebordoes.

exposed stonework on the walls, and large windows. Outside, there were two wells and a garden with space for a pool. The asking price was £122,500 'This is the most beautiful part of Minho and the house is finely situated on a hill. The windows opened onto fabulous views and we loved the exposed granite and limestone. It's very well modernized, as if no expense had been spared.' Pat could see the potential of the garden, envisaging arbors of black grapes and a pool on the sunny, elevated ground behind the house. An estimate from a local builder, who appreciated the need for care because of the slope of the hill, came in at £10,000. However, they decided on balance that the property was too small for them.

The beach resort of **MOLEDO** has long been a popular holiday destination for Portuguese politicians and football players. Thanks to its Atlantic coastline, the surf is reliable and there is an annual international beach games competition. Close to the border, there are spectacular views of the Spanish mountains beyond. Prices of properties by the coast tend to be around 50 per cent higher than those inland but the Motts found a modern, five-bedroom villa on the market for £115,000. It was much bigger that it first looked, and comprised an open, tiled living/dining room with a brick fireplace, a clean, white-tiled kitchen, three bathrooms, and good-sized bedrooms, one of which could be converted into a study. Outside, there was a vast balcony overlooking the Minho valley, ideal for eating out, and a narrow, but sunny garden. The Motts were impressed with the area and the spectacular views, as well as with the high standard of work on the house. It looked extremely good value for money and could have been a wise investment, since prices in the area were on the up. They were advised to spend an extra £2,500 on a structural survey to check that there would not be any subsidence due to the hill. Surveys are not automatically carried out in Portugal if a property is less than twenty years old. Neither Jim or Pat objected to the house being modern *per se*, but they did feel it lacked the soul they were hoping to find in a new home.

The modest façade of this five-bedroom villa near Moledo was deceptive.

Next, they travelled to the heart of the Lima valley to the well-preserved, medieval town of **PONTE DE LIMA** with its arching Roman bridge, imposing stone ramparts surrounding narrow streets, white houses and fifteenth-century palace in the centre. There is a weekly Monday market, first established in 1125, where haggling is an absolute must. The town even has its own beach on the banks of the river. In the centre, was a two-bedroom flat in a converted seventeenth-century building on the market for £97,000. It was on the first floor, consisting of a tiled corridor, a fully fitted kitchen/dining room, a living room and compact, tiled bathroom. It was furnished in typical Portuguese style with heavy mahogany furniture. It also had a terrace and small, raised garden containing mature fruit trees. 'We were impressed. The size was a surprise and we liked the layout. It's wonderfully positioned near the old Roman bridge and a stone's thrown from the beach. But it's not for us because of its limited outside space.'

Bent on finding the perfect garden, they turned to the countryside around the village of **ROMARIGAES**. Here, the land is green and fertile with hillsides rich in granite quarried for the traditional houses of Minho and for export. A 300-year-old restored farmhouse, covered with creepers, was for sale at £155,000. Full of character and lovingly restored, it had a square living room with a wooden floor and ceiling, hand-painted tiles surrounding the fireplace, a good-sized kitchen/dining room with a granite hearth, three bedrooms with different styles of wooden ceilings, an exposed-stone walled bathroom with a claw-foot bath, and a vast attic that could be turned into a fourth bedroom and another bathroom. Outside, there was a stone pool filled with natural spring water from the mountain, and a garden surrounded by agricultural land and trees. 'This is a house to fall in love with. It's so solidly built with stone and wood and has wonderful, high ceilings. The restoration is magnificent. Every detail has been considered so nothing jars with its original character.' In fact, the owner had been so thorough, that they felt central heating would spoil the style of the house so there was only a fire in the living room. If Pat and Jim were to buy, they would need to spend another £2500 to install a heating system in order to deal with the cold winters. 'This is a wonderful, rural, family house but we'd have to check whether there were any problems with the woodwork, and consider the added expense of insulation and heating. We loved it but we must think long and hard.'

Above: The Motts decided against the opportunity of living in Ponte de Lima because it meant they would not have enough outside space.
Below: A large country farmhouse with a history had been carefully restored near Romarigaes.

Think long and hard they did, and they came to the conclusion that it was 'too remote from civilization' and also rather too large for them to maintain from a distance. 'It was a bit of a dream house but not very practical if you're getting older. So we were sensible, which is rare for us!' They have decided to look in Spain, along the coast south of Barcelona. Friendly people and pretty villages are not enough for them; Pat and Jim want to be near to a town that can also offer them the theatre, opera and the arts. 'That sort of thing doesn't matter if you're on holiday. But if we lived there, we would miss it.' But they still love Portugal and all it offers, so would they be interested if a wonderful property were to come up? 'Yes, we'd certainly still be tempted.'

Ex-pats

Lisbon
Bob Hughes

To go or not to go? That was the question confronting Bob Hughes when the company he worked for went bust in 1991. For six years he had worked without a single holiday, supplying equipment to hotels and guesthouses in the UK. He had a distant memory of a holiday he had once spent in the Algarve's Quateira away from the drunken Brits. That was enough to get him into his Fiat camper and onto the road.

When he arrived at Quateira, however, it was not how he remembered. 'Where there had only been a few apartment blocks was now developed beyond recognition. The first night I was woken by drunks so left the next day to find peace and tranquillity up the coast at Zambujeira do Mar – to visit this place is a must.' While he was there, he heard of a British man who had bought some land in the Alentejo and was trying to restore it to how it once was. 'Getting rid of thousands of eucalyptus trees to make way for cork oaks and wild pigs is no easy task. I worked there voluntarily, running a work camp for British students before I was offered a paid job helping to renovate two farmhouses for a British ex-pat from the Sintra area near Lisbon.' This was when he first fell in love with the Alentejo and its local inhabitants. 'I remember my first Christmas day, spent in the home of a young Alentejo family armed with my Portuguese/English dictionary. I couldn't put more than two words together in those days, but I soon discovered that it was no use refusing a glass of wine because you'd be given one anyway.' During that time, Bob made many Portuguese friends who he still sees to this day. When the work was finished he moved to Lisbon, working on projects for the same employer.

He met Sónia, an English-speaking Portuguese woman, who was teaching at the International School. In 1996, after three years together, they were planning to get married when Bob had a heart attack and a triple by-pass operation. 'After a rest, I was ready for new challenges, so got into the bureaucracy of marriage and then started

Bob Hughes has enjoyed living in Portugal since he took a chance and left England over ten years ago.

Bob has settled in the city of Lisbon, a busy metropolis that boasts atmospheric historical and modern districts.

training and working for a Real Estate Agency in the Cascais area of Lisbon. It was extremely rewarding, but I felt there wasn't enough attention paid to the important person, the client.' With enough experience under his belt, Bob decided to go it alone and set up his own company. It was not easy, but with a competent accountant, who set up the company, registering it with the government agency that controls real estate activities, it took off. Keeping the company small enables Bob to offer his clients the personal service that he had felt was missing in his previous job. He sells both to Portuguese and foreign buyers, and organizes rentals for foreigners, too. After his first year in business, he was introduced to AFPOP (Association of Foreign Property Owners in Portugal), an association geared to helping foreigners living or working in Portugal. He is now the Lisbon area representative and also a member of the Management Council. 'I see helping other foreigners overcoming their everyday problems of living here as my greatest achievement since I came to Portugal. What was it that kept me here? (No, it was not just the sun!) It was the friendliness of the average Portuguese anywhere outside the major cities. What do I dislike? The fact that once settled into the driver's seat of a car, most Portuguese are hell-bent on getting it to go as fast as possible and getting it to stop takes a lot less consideration, hence the awful driving statistics. Most foreigners will find, once over the bureaucracy and the slowness of achieving results, living in Portugal is less stressful and calmer. My three weeks holiday has stretched to eleven years this May!'

Ex-pats

Algarve
José and Edwin Boothby

Five years ago, José and Edwin Boothby were happily retired and living in Gloucestershire, when a friend suggested they take their caravans to spend the winter together in Portugal. 'We had never taken the caravan abroad before but we agreed, then panicked.' After studying maps and taking advice from friends, they set off that January. Having crossed the Spanish border, they found a campsite in Vila Nova de Caçela and after four months were so smitten with the country and the friendliness of the people that they decided to move there for good. They returned the following September, travelling the length of the Algarve to make sure they had chosen the right area. 'We wanted a quieter life than exists on the coast, and all around Caçela is very rural (we've always lived in the country), very Portuguese, and extremely beautiful.'

Neither of them knew how to go about finding a house, but the local hairdresser put José in touch with an estate agent. They quickly realized they could not afford anything as nice as they had in the UK but began to consider buying land and building to their own design: 'Eventually we chose this plot because we didn't want to be too remote, a bus comes to the local bar twice a day, there's a shop that opens on request and views are spectacular. We thought we'd lose it because we had to sell our English house first but our agent said, "I shook your hand. I don't go back on my word. I'll save it for you."'

Within three days of returning to the UK, the Boothbys had a buyer for their house and organized a garage sale to get rid of all the belongings they no longer needed. After this, it took one month to buy the land with the help of a local solicitor, move their caravan to the site and to begin planning. The agent's husband project-managed the building work with an architect he had worked with before. The Boothbys looked at some of their previous work, and then specified three bedrooms, a roof terrace and a large kitchen, and sat back to watch their house take shape over nine months. 'We were warned that it would take much longer and have since seen friends have terrible problems with builders. But we were fortunate in our project manager who knew the council and all the local procedures. We've found it's not what but who you know that gets things done here.' What is more, it came in at the estimated cost of £75,000 (including the land).

Something particularly striking about their move has been the sheer warmth of their welcome into the village. Once, after a hard

A caravan holiday in Portugal was enough to convince the Boothbys that they wanted to sell up and move there for good.

Above and below: Unable to find anything within their budget as comfortable as their English home, the Boothbys decided to buy a plot of land and design a house of their own.

morning's gardening, José looked up to see her neighbour and two children offering them lunch from the barbecue with wine and bread. After the annual Christmas pig-killing, they were the only outsiders to be asked to their neighbour's celebratory family party. They are frequently given vegetables, eggs and buckets of lemons. In exchange, José gives away her home-made lemon curd and bunches of sweet peas, as well as making and selling découpage cards and pictures in local craft fairs. 'It's wonderful to be able to share these things with the Portuguese, who haven't come across them before.' Meanwhile, as a retired heating engineer, Edwin enjoys using his talents at fixing things for people. Over the last year they have been taking private Portuguese lessons. 'It's very difficult, but we can have small conversations with neighbours and go shopping now.' They have joined the Portuguese health service, have private health insurance – useful when Edwin needed a cataract operation – and receive their British pension. 'The cost of living is so reasonable that we live very comfortably here.' Other English people living in the area have become friends, but perhaps their best moments are those shared with the two stray dogs that they rescued. 'When we walk with them across the hills, we could be the only people in the world. We love the life we have here and so far all our expectations have been fulfilled.'

France

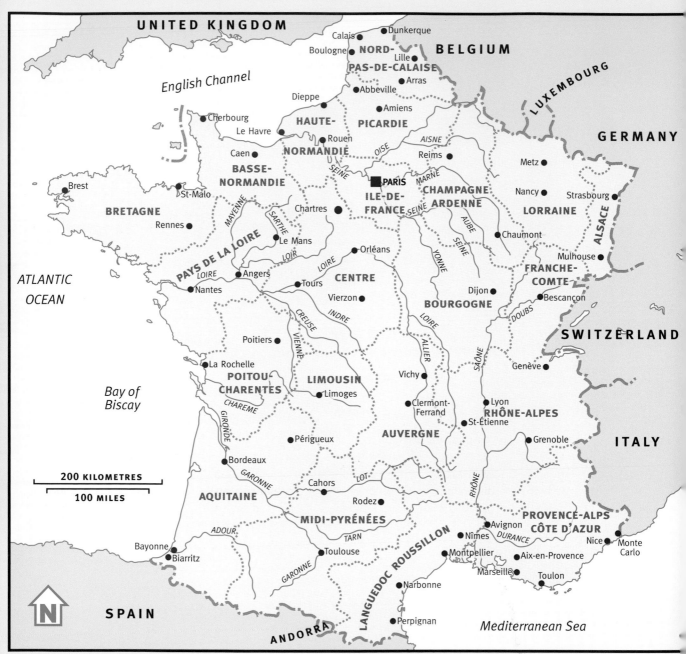

UNITED KINGDOM

English Channel

BELGIUM

LUXEMBOURG

GERMANY

ATLANTIC OCEAN

Bay of Biscay

SWITZERLAND

ITALY

SPAIN

ANDORRA

Mediterranean Sea

Calais · **Dunkerque**
Boulogne · **NORD-** **Lille**
PAS-DE-CALAIS
Arras
Dieppe **Abbeville**
Cherbourg **Amiens**
Le Havre **HAUTE-** **PICARDIE**
NORMANDIE **Rouen** *OISE* **Reims**
Caen *SEINE* **Metz**
BASSE- **ILE-DE-** *MARNE* **Nancy** **Strasbourg**
NORMANDIE **PARIS** **CHAMPAGNE** **LORRAINE**
Brest **FRANCE** **ARDENNE** **ALSACE**
St-Malo **Chartres** *SEINE* **Chaumont**
BRETAGNE *AUBE* **Mulhouse**
Rennes *MAYENNE* *SARTHE* *YONNE* **FRANCHE-**
Le Mans **Orléans** **COMTE**
PAYS DE LA LOIRE *LOIR* *LOIRE* **Dijon** **Bescançon**
Angers **CENTRE** *SEINE* *DOUBS*
Nantes **Tours** **BOURGOGNE**
LOIRE **Vierzon** *LOIRE*
CREUSE *INDRE* *SAÔNE*
Poitiers *VIENNE* *ALLIER* **Genève**
La Rochelle **Vichy** **Lyon**
POITOU **LIMOUSIN** **Clermont-** **RHÔNE-ALPES**
CHARENTES **Limoges** **Ferrand** **St-Étienne**
CHARENTE **AUVERGNE** **Grenoble**
Périgueux *RHÔNE*
GIRONDE
Bordeaux
GARONNE **Cahors** *LOT* **Rodez**
AQUITAINE **PROVENCE-ALPS**
MIDI-PYRÉNÉES **Avignon** **CÔTE D'AZUR**
ADOUR *TARN* **Nîmes** *DURANCE* **Nice**
Bayonne *GARONNE* **Toulouse** **Montpellier** **Monte**
Biarritz **Aix-en-Provence** **Carlo**
LANGUEDOC ROUSSILLON **Marseille** **Toulon**
Narbonne
Perpignan

200 KILOMETRES
100 MILES

N

CORSICA

Bastia

Ajaccio

France

In recent years, thousands have left crowded Britain behind to enjoy the uncomplicated life of a settler in rural France. There are plenty of desirable properties available, whether your fantasy is an ornate chateau surrounded by its own grounds, or just a humble cottage needing a facelift. At least 500,000 Britons already own French property, either as their primary residence or a second home. They have come because they love good food and wine, the French approach to art and culture, the excellent facilities for rambling, messing about in boats, outdoor sports and adventures, even shopping and, of course, a more hospitable climate. But, for many, the fundamental idea is simply to relax and let life flow by.

France covers almost twice the geographical area of the United Kingdom, but travelling there has never been easier. The recent expansion of low-cost airlines means there are flights to provincial airports, which in turn give fast access to some of the lesser-known regions such as Burgundy, Auvergne or Limousin, Charente and Brittany, as well as to long-term British favourites, such as Provence, Dordogne, and the Alps. Rail travel is state-subsidized and highly efficient, especially the excellent TGV (*train à grande vitesse*) train network, which now covers most of the country, and includes a new, fast line from Paris to Marseilles. France also boasts a first-class motorway system, which the motorist joins immediately after crossing the channel either by sea or tunnel.

The regions within France are fascinating in their variety and, for selling up and moving across permanently, the choice of where to look is enormous. However, for second-home purchasers wanting to visit their property from Britain at weekends as well as for longer holidays, it is important to remember that being forced to travel long distances, on either or both sides of the Channel, can eventually make the attractions of a weekend hideaway pall. So be realistic and limit your search-area to regions closest to the UK – Brittany and Normandy or, if you are drawn to French metropolitan life and your budget will stretch that far, to Paris or to somewhere in easy reach of an airport.

regions

The different regions of France offer a considerable range of climates, landscapes, activities and attractions. The French are a nation justifiably proud of their history and heritage. Evidence of the country's rich and varied past is found in ancient neolithic monuments, picturesque medieval villages and great historic cities, impressive chateaux and cathedrals. Long associated with arts and culture, France has produced numerous men of letters, artists and scientists, whose influence has spread throughout the world. There are over 5,000 festivals that take place throughout the year. Some are international, others local. Some are religious pageants, others celebrate a local harvest or other particular events. Everywhere there are daily markets selling fresh produce, and you find *brocantes* (second-hand shops) and flea markets in most provincial towns. France produces over 350 different cheeses, hundreds of thousands of different wines and an unparalleled cuisine, with a multitude of regional specialities relying on high-quality local produce. It is only possible to outline the richness and diversity of the pleasures that lie in store.

facts

CAPITAL: Paris
AREA: 547,030 sq km
COASTLINE: 3,427 km
POPULATION: 59,520,000
CURRENCY: Euro
TIME ZONE: GMT + 1 hour
ELECTRICITY: 220 volts
WEIGHTS AND MEASURES: metric
RELIGION: mainly Roman Catholic
LANGUAGE: French
GOVERNMENT: Republic
INTERNATIONAL DIALLING CODE: 00 33
INDEPENDENCE: 486
NATIONAL HOLIDAY: Bastille Day, 14 July

Alsace

DEPARTMENTS: Haut-Rhin, Bas-Rhin
LANDSCAPE: thick forests and fertile agricultural land, picture-postcard villages, vine-clad hillsides
MAJOR TOWNS: Strasbourg (capital), Colmar, Mulhouse
HIGHLIGHTS: wine route, Strasbourg cathedral, white storks of Hunawihr, Parc Naturel Régional des Ballons des Vosges
FESTIVALS: *Festival International de Musique* (Strasbourg, June/July), *Festival Jazz* (Strasbourg, July), *Marchés de Noel* (Strasbourg, Colmar, December), *Foire Régional des Vins d'Alsace* (Colmar, August)
HANDICRAFTS: pottery, glasswork, woodcarving, weaving, painting
FOOD: *choucroute, pâté de foie gras en croute,* goose, pheasant, hare, German sausages including *saucisse de Strasbourg, boeuf salé* (smoked beef), *tarte flambé*
DRINK: white wine – Riesling, Gewurztraminer and Tokay-Pinot Gris; beer; Kirsch; Poire William (eau de vie)
AIRPORT: Strasbourg

Aquitaine

DEPARTMENTS: Dordogne, Gironde, Landes, Lot-et-Garonne, Pyrénées-Atlantiques
LANDSCAPE: from Atlantic coastline to rugged forests in the south, rolling country-side threaded with rivers in the north-east
MAJOR TOWNS: Bordeaux, Perigueux, Mont de Marsan, Pau, Biarritz
HIGHLIGHTS: fortified medieval *bastide* villages, hilltop chateaux, Lascaux caves, Arcachon sand dune
FESTIVALS: Espelette Red Pepper Festival (October), oyster festivals (Arcachon basin, summer), Sea Festival (Arcachon, August), Salt Festival (Salies des Bearne, September)
HANDICRAFTS: basketwork, shepherds' crooks, Basque linen and berets, Bayonne chocolate, Noutron knives
FOOD: *foie gras,* truffles, Bayonne ham, *piperade,* goose, duck
DRINK: red wine – Bordeaux, Haut Médoc, Margaux, St Emilion and Pomerol; white wine – Entre-Deux-Mers; dessert wine – Sauternes
AIRPORT: Biarritz

Auvergne

DEPARTMENTS: Allier, Cantal, Haute-Loire, Puy de Dome
LANDSCAPE: spectacular, volcanic landscape, lakes, and the fertile plain of Le Limagne
MAJOR TOWNS: Clermont-Ferrand, Aurillac, Le Puy en Velay, Moulins, Vichy
HIGHLIGHTS: Parc Naturel Régional des Volcans d'Auvergne, Parc Naturel Régional du Livradois-Forez, Romanesque churches, thermal springs, Vulcania (a scientific exploration park), castles at La Palisse and Murol
FESTIVALS: *Fêtes Renaissance du Roi l'Oiseau* (Le Puy en Velay, September), Aurillac street festival (August), *Fête de la cerise* (Vieillevie, June), *Fête de la Fourme* (St Martin Valmeroux, September)
HANDICRAFTS: lace, the Thiers knife, umbrellas
FOOD: cheeses – Cantal, Bleu d'Auvergne and St Nectaire; tripe; *potée* (vegetable soup)
DRINK: Côtes d'Auvergne wine, Salers (liqueur)
AIRPORT: Clermont-Ferrand-Aulnat

Burgundy

DEPARTMENTS: Côte d'Or, Saône et Loire, Nièvre, Yonne
LANDSCAPE: fertile landscape with internationally renowned vineyards
MAJOR TOWNS: Dijon, Nevers, Mâcon, Auxerre
HIGHLIGHTS: Dijon, Hôtel-Dieu des Hospices in Beaune, Morvan Regional Nature Park, Romanesque architecture at Fontenay and Vézelay
FESTIVALS: *Saint-Vincent tournant* (January, *Fête de la Vigne* (Dijon, August–September), music festival of Mersault, medieval festival of Semur-An-Auxois, many regional food fairs
FOOD: mustard, Bourgogne snails, Charolais beef, Bresse chicken
DRINK: red wine – Gevrey-Chambertin, Bourgogne, Mercurey and Beaune; white wine – Chablis and Mâcon-Villages
AIRPORT: Dijon

Brittany

DEPARTMENTS: Côtes-d'Armor, Finistère, Ille-et-Vilaine, Morbihan
LANDSCAPE: rugged coastline with rolling wooded hills, fields and moors inland
MAJOR TOWNS: Quimper, Vannes, Dinan, Rennes
HIGHLIGHTS: standing stones at Carnac, Fougères castle, Vitré castle, Océanopolis (Brest)
FESTIVALS: *Festival Interceltique* (Lorient, August), *Festival de Cornouaille* (Quimper,

Well-preserved half-timbered houses in Colmar's canal quarter, 'Petit Venise'.

July), Fête des Filets Bleus (Concarneau, August), Fête des Ramparts (Dinan, September)

HANDICRAFTS: lace, embroidery, *faience* (glazed earthenware), jewellery, Breton clothing
FOOD: crêpes, galettes, seafood (especially oysters and mussels)
DRINK: cider
AIRPORTS: Rennes, Brest, Dinard
PORTS: St Malo, Roscoff

Centre/Val de Loire

DEPARTMENTS: Cher, Eure-et-Loire, Indre, Indre-et-Loire, Loiret
LANDSCAPE: luxuriant valleys
MAJOR TOWNS: Orléans, Chartres, Blois, Tours, Chateauroux, Bourges
HIGHLIGHTS: magnificent chateaux, home of Leonardo da Vinci (Amboise), son-et-lumières (Chateau d'Azay le Rideau, Chateau de Blois)
FESTIVALS: Fêtes Romantiques (Nohant, June), International Organ Festival(Chartres, June–July)
HANDICRAFTS: porcelain, ceramics, pottery, stained glass, jewellery
FOOD: goat's cheese, *tarte tatin*, *pithiviers* (almond pastries), *cotignac* (quince preserve), river fish, game, *coq en barbouille* (chicken)
DRINK: red wine – Chinon and Bourgueil; white wine – Sancerre and Quincy
AIRPORTS: Tours, Bourges, Poitiers

Brittany's granite cottages are popular among British buyers looking for a convenient weekend retreat.

Champagne-Ardenne

DEPARTMENTS: Ardenne, Aube, Marne, Haute-Marne
LANDSCAPE: agricultural plains and lakes in the south, and forested hills in the north
MAJOR TOWNS: Chalons-sur-Marne, Charleville-Mézières, Troyes, Chaumont
HIGHLIGHTS: Reims cathedral, champagne-tasting in Epernay, museums in Troyes, Parc Naturel Régional de la Forêt de l'Orient, the Champagne route
FESTIVALS: *Les Folies Médiévales* (St Dizier, May/June), *Fêtes Johanniques* (Reims, June), *Les Sacres du Folklore* (Reims, June)
HANDICRAFTS: wickerwork, cutlery and precision instruments, crystal glass making
FOOD: *andouillettes* (sausages), Ardennes ham, Chaource and Langres cheeses
DRINK: Champagne (white/rosé); Bouzy Rouge (red wine)
AIRPORT: Reims-Champagne

Corse (Corsica)

DEPARTMENTS: Corse du Sud, Haut Corsica
LANDSCAPE: wild beauty, from mountains and forests to scrubland and sandy beaches
MAJOR TOWN: Ajaccio
HIGHLIGHTS: Romanesque churches, megalithic stone warriors (Filitosa)
FESTIVALS: Rencontres Polyphoniques (Calvi, September), Sea Festival (Salinzara, May), Catennaciu (Sartene, Good Friday), Napoleon festivals (Ajaccio, August), Strana Vela (old sailing boats, Calvi, October/November), Festival of the Wind (Calvi, October)
HANDICRAFTS: metalwork, woodwork, woollen produce, basketry, pottery
FOOD: porkmeats, *azziminu* (fish soup), citrus fruits, chestnuts, sheep's cheese, sweet pastries
DRINK: red and white wine – Vin de Pays de l'Ile de Beauté and Ajaccio; liqueur – Cap Corse
AIRPORTS: Ajaccio, Calvi, Bastia, Figari

Franche-Comté

DEPARTMENTS: Doubs, Haute Sâone, Territoire de Belfort, Jura
LANDSCAPE: rolling farmland and Alpine scenery
MAJOR TOWNS: Besançon, Belfort, Vesoul, Lons-le-Saunier
HIGHLIGHTS: clock museum (Besançon), the Jura mountains, the Vallé de la Loue, Le

Corbusier's church at Ronchamp
FESTIVALS: sausage festival (Morteau, August), Blueberry Festival (Frasne, August), International Festival of Music (Besançon, September), Montbéliard Chocolate Festival (October)
FOOD: mountain cheeses, including Vacherin and Comté, Morteau sausage
DRINK: red and white wine – Vin de Pays de Franche Comté, Côtes du Jura, Château Chalon, L'Etoile

Ile de France

DEPARTMENTS: Ville de Paris, Seine-et-Marne, Yvelines, Essonne, Hauts-de-Seine, Seine-St-Denis, Val-et-Marne, Val d'Oise
LANDSCAPE: tapestry of forests, arable fields and plains with the country's capital at its heart
MAJOR TOWNS: Paris, Versailles, Pontoise, Melun
HIGHLIGHTS: Paris, Château de Fontainebleu, Forêt de Fontainebleu, Château de Versailles, Disneyland Paris
FESTIVALS: *Banlieues Blues* (Paris, February/March), *Foire de Paris* (April/May), Paris Jazz Festival (May/September)
FOOD: Brie de Meaux, Groslay pears, apples from Saint Germain-de-Laye, mushrooms
AIRPORTS: Orly, Charles de Gaulle, Beauvais

Languedoc-Rousillon

DEPARTMENTS: Aude, Gard, Herault, Lozere, Pyrenees-Orientales
LANDSCAPE: mountainous (foothills of the Pyrenees), with a Mediterranean coastline, and vineyards further inland
MAJOR TOWNS: Montpellier, Perpignan, Nîmes, Bézier
HIGHLIGHTS: Carcassone, Vernet-les-Bains, Cathar castles, Pont du Gard (Roman aqueduct), Uzès, Parc National des Cévennes
FESTIVALS: *Festival de la Cité* (Carcassone, July), *Foire à l'Ail* (Uzès, June), Truffle Fair (Uzès, January) *Fête des Vendanges*, (Carcassonne, October), *Printemps du Jazz* (Nimes, March), local *corridas* and *ferias* (February, June, September), Pablo Casals Festival (Prades, July)
HANDICRAFTS: jewellery (garnets), pottery, stonework, basketwork, textiles, glassware, denim
FOOD: *cassoulet* (stew), Roquefort cheese, seafood, *tellines* (little clams), *Ttoro* (fish stew), sausages, smoked hams, *la boeuf gardiane*
DRINK: red wine – Vin de Pays d'Oc, Corbières,

Coteax du Languedoc, Minervois and Faugères
AIRPORTS: Perpignan, Nîmes

Limousin

DEPARTMENTS: Corrèze, Creuse, Haute-Vienne
LANDSCAPE: unspoiled, undulating countryside with livestock farming and many rivers and lakes
MAJOR TOWNS: Limoges, Gueret, Tulle
HIGHLIGHTS: Vézère valley, Limoges cathedral, medieval villages, Limousin cows
HANDICRAFTS: porcelain, enamel and lace (Limoges), tapestries, carpets (Aubusson)
FESTIVALS: National Festival of Music (Bellac, June/July), Fête des Ponts (Limoges, June), Fête de la Framboise (Concèze, June)
FOOD: salted buckwheat pancakes, potato pie, pigs' trotters, sweet chestnut cake, beef
AIRPORT: Poitiers

Lorraine

DEPARTMENTS: Meurthe-et-Moselle, Muese, Moselle, Vosges
LANDSCAPE: wooded hills and river valleys, and heavily industrial in some areas
MAJOR TOWNS: Nancy, Metz, Epinal, Bar-le-Duc
HIGHLIGHTS: Place Stanislas and Musée de l'Ecole de Nancy, Metz Cathedral, World War One battle fields (Verdun), thermal waters
HANDICRAFTS: faience (glazed earthenware), lace, embroidery, musical instruments
FESTIVALS: Carnavas (Sarreguemines, February), Fête mediévale (Gondrecourt le Château, June), Fête de la Mirabelle (Metz, August), Jass Pulsations (Nancy, October)
FOOD: *cassoulet* (stew), *choucroute garnie* (sauerkraut with cold meats), *quiche Lorraine*, *tarte flambé*, *grillade à la champagneules* (ham and cheese on toast), Munster cheese, macaroons
DRINK: white wine – Côtes de Toul and Vins de Moselle, beer
AIRPORT: Metz-Nancy-Lorraine

Midi-Pyrenees

DEPARTMENTS: Ariege, Aveyron, Haute-Garonne, Gers, Lot, Hautes-Pyrenees, Tarn, Tarn-et-Garonne
LANDSCAPE: from mountain scenery of the Pyrenees to the dramatic Lot Valley in the north
MAJOR TOWNS: Toulouse, Foix, Auch, Tarbes,

Vallauris is among the many picturesque Provençal villages that continue to attract British buyers.

Montauban, Cahors, Rodez
HIGHLIGHTS: Lourdes, Montauban museum, Aérospatiale and the Cité de l'Espace museum (Toulouse), Musée Toulouse Lautrec (Albi), *bastide* towns
FESTIVALS: *Festival Garonne* (Toulouse, July), *Musique d'Eté* (Toulouse, July/August), *Festival Albi-Jazz* (Albi, June), *Carnaval* (Albi, Lent), *Fête des 400 Coups* (Montauban, September)
HANDICRAFTS: lambskin gloves, boxing gloves, parfum de toilette
FOOD: *foie gras*, *cassoulet* (stew), Laucanes sausages, Roquefort cheese
DRINK: Armagnac; red wine – Côtes du Roussillon and Collioure; dessert wine – Maury and Rivesaltes
AIRPORTS: Toulouse, Carcassonne

Nord-Pas-de-Calais

DEPARTMENTS: Nord, Pas-de-Calais
LANDSCAPE: industrial (although industry is in decline), beaches, dunes, cliffs
MAJOR TOWNS: Calais, Bologne-sur-Mer, Lille
HIGHLIGHTS: Côte d'Opale, Nausicca (centre for marine environment), Furet du Nord (Europe's biggest bookshop)
FESTIVALS: *Fêtes de Lille* (June), *Festival Mozart* (Lille, November/March)
FOOD: seafood
DRINK: beer
PORTS: Calais, Dunkirk, Le Touquet

Normandy

DEPARTMENTS: Calvados, Manche, Orne (Basse-Normandie), Eure, Seine Maritime (Haute-Normandie)
LANDSCAPE: 'bocage' agricultural land, orchards and pastures
MAJOR TOWNS: Cherbourg, Caen, Rouen, Dieppe
HIGHLIGHTS: Bayeux Tapestry, Monet's Garden at Giverny, Mont St-Michel, D-Day landings' beaches, Etretat cliffs
FESTIVALS: American Film Festival (Deauville, September), *Festival Folklorique* (Trouville, June), Apple Fair (Vimoutiers, October), Herring Fair (Lierey, November), Horse Festival (Calvados, October)
HANDICRAFTS: lace, copper crafts, porcelain
FOOD: Camembert, *tripe à la mode de Caen*, seafood, *bonhomme Normand* (duck in cider and cream), galantine, *poulet vallée d'Auge* (chicken with cream)
DRINK: Calvados (apple brandy), cider, pommeau (apple liqueur)
AIRPORT: Caen

PORTS: Le Havre, Dieppe, Cherbourg, Caen (Oouistram)

Pays de la Loire

DEPARTMENTS: Loire-Atlantique, Maine-et-Loire, Mayenne, Sarthe, Vendée
LANDSCAPE: from beaches with white sand and sand dunes and salt marshes, to pine woods and fertile valleys
MAJOR TOWNS: Angers, Nantes, Le Mans, Laval, La Roche-sur-Yon
HIGHLIGHTS: châteaux (Chambord, Chaumont, Cheverny), and vineyards
HANDICRAFTS: furniture, textiles, clothing
FESTIVALS: *Fête Johaniques* (Orleans, May), Marche Rabelais (Chinon, August)
FOOD: *andouillettes* (chitterling sausages) *rillettes* (potted pork), *tarte tatin*, freshwater fish, poultry
DRINK: white wine – Muscadet, Grosplant (dry); red and white wines – Anjou, Fiefs Vendéens; dessert wine – Coteaux du Layon
AIRPORT: Nantes-Atlantique

Picardie

DEPARTMENTS: Aisne, Oise, Somme
LANDSCAPE: flat agricultural land with some industry
MAJOR TOWNS: Amiens, Beauvais, Laon
HIGHLIGHTS: memorials to battle of the Somme, cathedrals at Beauvais, Laon, Amiens, prehistoric sites, Château de Pierrefonds, Parc Asterix, Chantilly
FESTIVALS: Soft Fruit Festival (Noyon, July), Fête de la Quiche (Mirecourt, May), Hot Air Balloon festival (Lille and Vittel, May)
HANDICRAFTS: tapestries, wooden puppets, furniture, stained glass, gold and silversmiths
FOOD: *ficelle Picardie* (ham and mushroom crêpe), duck pâté, Maroilles cheese, smoked eel, macaroons, Tuiles amiénoises (chocolate)
DRINK: Champagne, beer
AIRPORT: Beauvais

Poitou-Charentes

DEPARTMENTS: Charente, Charente-Maritime, Deux-Sevres, Vienne
LANDSCAPE: white, sandy beaches, salt marshes, wooded inland with arable and livestock pastures
MAJOR TOWNS: La Rochelle, Poitiers, Niort, Angoulème
HIGHLIGHTS: Île de Re, Aubeterre, Futuroscope (Museum of the Future)
FESTIVALS: *Francofolies* (La Rochelle, July),

Festival International du Film (La Rochelle, June/July), Confolens International Festival of Folklore (August)

FOOD: seafood, mushroom *fricassée*, venison, Charolais veal

DRINK: Vins du Haut Poitou (white/red wine), Vins de Pays Charentais (white wine), Cognac, Pineau de Charentes (liqueur)

AIRPORTS: Poitiers, La Rochelle

Provence-Alpes-Côte d'Azur

DEPARTMENTS: Alpes-de-Haute-Provence, Hautes-Alpes, Alpes-Maritimes, Bouches-du-Rhone, Var, Vaucluse

LANDSCAPE: beaches and blue seas in the Côte d'Azur, and densely wooded hills further inland

MAJOR TOWNS: Aix-en-Provence, Marseilles, Monaco, Arles, Avignon, Nice, Cannes, Toulon

HIGHLIGHTS: Roman theatre at Orange, Gorges du Verdon, French Riviera, perched villages, Palais des Papes (Avignon), Basilique Notre Dame de la Garde (Marseille), Village des Bories, Camargue

FESTIVALS: *Festival Provencal d'Aix et du Pays d'Aix* (July), *Festival d'Avignon* (July/August), *Les Rencontres Internationales de la Photographie* (Arles, July), *Fête d'Arles* (June/July), bullfighting (Arles, Easter to September), *Festival de Nice* (Mardi Gras, Shrove Tuesday), Nice jazz festival (July), Cannes film festival (May), Lemon Festival (Menton, February)

FOOD: *bouillabaisse* (fish soup), *pissaladière* (like pizza), *salade niçoise*, olives, olive oil

DRINK: red wine – Côtes du Lubéron, Bandol, Gigondas, Vacqueyras and Châteauneuf du Pape; dessert wine – Beaumes de Venise

AIRPORTS: Marseilles-Provence, Avignon-Caumont, Nîmes-Arles-Camargue, Aeroport International Nice-Côte d'Azur

Rhone-Alpes

DEPARTMENTS: Ain, Ardeche, Drome, Isère, Loire, Rhone, Savoie, Haute-Savoie

LANDSCAPE: green and hilly around Lyon, with the Alps from Lake Geneva up to Mont Blanc

MAJOR TOWNS: Lyon, Annecy, Grenoble, Chamonix

HIGHLIGHTS: Mont Blanc, Baume-les-Messieurs (waterfalls and caves)

FESTIVALS: *Les Nuits de Fourvières* (Lyon, June/September), *Fête des Lumières* (Lyon, December), *Biennale de la Danse* (Lyon, September)

FOOD: *andouillettes à la Lyonnaise*, frogs, *rosette de Lyons* (sauasages), *tartiflette* (potatoes and local cheese), *gratins de crozet* (locally made pasta and cheese), Emmental cheese, fondue

DRINK: red wine – Beaujolais, Fleurie, Hermitage and Mondeuse; white wine – Apremont; Poiret, Chartreuse

AIRPORTS: Lyon-St-Exupery, St Etienne, Annecy, Lyon-Satolas

An Alpine chalet has excellent rental potential since, if well located, it will be in demand in both winter and summer.

Property

During the 1990s, the French property market floundered due to the world recession but has stabilized, with prices generally rising between 5 and 10 per cent a year since then. However, over the last two or three years prices have risen by an extraordinary 25 to 40 per cent in some areas. Despite that alarming statistic, it is still perfectly possible to find property that is far better value for money than in the UK. Areas that have long been popular with British home owners abroad are Brittany and Normandy, which are so accessible from the UK, Provence and the Côte d'Azur, with their balmy climate, and the Dordogne or 'little England' with its attractive architecture, lush landscape and mild weather. Paris and the French Alps are the other two price hot spots. Pas de Calais, Charente, the Pyrénées Atlantiques, the Landes, Lot and Gers are fast catching up in popularity, offering similar attractions. Improved road and train links, and the proliferation of low-cost airlines flying to smaller, local airports have opened the country up, making it easier for foreign buyers to reach regions, which have until recently been quite inaccessible. Recently, Languedoc-Roussillon, Limousin, Mayenne and the Vendée have been up and coming. In addition to this, house hunters are beginning to venture into previously

Towns perched on rocky outcrops in Languedoc Roussillon make remote getaways for the busy city dweller.

unexploited areas, such as Burgundy, the Auvergne, Aveyron and Lozére.

Inevitably, property prices are highest in the regions where the demand is greatest, although there are variations, according to the location and condition of properties. Holiday houses near the Atlantic and Mediterranean coasts, major towns (especially Paris) and attractions will command more interest and therefore be more expensive than those in areas off the beaten track. If you are searching for that rural idyll – an isolated, picturesque, old house with a little of its own land, perhaps a swimming pool and lovely panoramic views – then France can almost certainly provide it.

The first half of the nineteenth century saw the French countryside at the height of its prosperity, but then an epidemic of phylloxera decimated the vineyards and began a process of rural depopulation. Following this, many peasant lives were lost during the Franco-Prussian War and the two World Wars. With the continuing growth of French industry and technology in the last century and the increased mechanization of farming, farms and hamlets were gradually deserted, and villages declined as the remaining population decamped to the towns to find work and a viable living. This left numerous rural properties unoccupied, many of which fell into disrepair. Restoring them has been hugely popular with second-home owners, both French and foreign, who relish the opportunity to relieve the pressures of city life. Today, there are still plenty of old properties to be found in France, whether ruined or partially, or fully, renovated.

The long house (*longère*) is one of the oldest styles of architecture – a long, single-storey building characterized by its thick walls, small windows and large hearth. They were originally inhabited by a family and their livestock, who lived at opposite ends from one another, the animal's end having a slightly sloping floor to drain away the liquid manure. There would have been several external doors giving access to the different areas. During the eighteenth century, the design was enlarged, and rooms were added in the roof space, with dormer and gable-end windows for light. They are especially typical of Brittany, Normandy, Mayenne and Anjou, although they can also be found further south.

Once the property of wealthy merchants or village leaders, the *salle haute* (high house) became popular further down the social hierarchy during the nineteenth century. The ground floor was used for storage or production, with living accommodation on the floor above. Usually, an outside staircase and landing joined the two, both protected by overhanging eaves and supported by pillars. Often, the gable end of the house faces the street. Houses like this are to be found mostly in southern regions, where they may also have a *pigeonnière* (dovecote), especially in the Lot. Styles vary according to region but *pigeonnières* are found built from stone or half-timbered, round or square, with nests from floor to ceiling or only in the upper part, leaving the lower part free for storage.

Over the years, abandoned farmhouses (*fermes* or *fermettes*, depending on their size) have enjoyed a considerable vogue as subjects for restoration. Farmhouses rarely date back further than the nineteenth century, and their architecture varies from region to region, depending on the local building materials. For example, the solid, Provençal *mas* (grange) has a gently sloping pantiled roof, supported by stone walls often rendered in ochre or beige, with asymmetrically arranged doors and windows. They are often seen joined to outbuildings of differing heights. Many farmhouses throughout the country were built around a courtyard with barns, stables and other outbuildings attached or separate. These are particularly in demand by those intending to convert the outbuildings into *gîtes* for holiday letting. Landscape and climate were important factors for determining design. Farmhouses in the south-west of France, particularly in the Landes and Basque country, were oriented against the harsh Atlantic winds, with steeply pitched protective roofs on one side, frequently reaching lower on that side than the other, sheltering the family, their livestock, harvested crops and tools. In the Auvergne, the farmhouses have tiny windows to protect the inhabitants against harsh winters. The interplay of shape and function is seen at work again in the wooden Alpine chalets (their roofs pitched less sharply, their balconies decoratively carved) which make comfortable holiday homes for winter-sports fanatics. Remember, it is best to buy a chalet in the summer, when any defects are not hidden beneath inches of snow.

The *maisons de maître* (master's houses) were originally for the upper classes, but during the eighteenth and nineteenth centuries farmers and wine-growers began to build them for themselves. They are usually two or three storeys high, and double-fronted, with dormer windows in the eaves. A *vigneron* house would have once belonged to a prosperous wine-grower and can be found complete with the old wine

Arcaded medieval lanes and an impressive sixteenth century château combine to make Gordes one of the most visited towns in Provence.

presses in the cellar or outhouse. A *manoir* (manor house) on the other hand, is a grander, two-storey country house with its own land, that was lived in by the *seigneur* and his family, usually surrounded by its own grounds, their grandeur reflecting the size and profitability of the estate. A *gentilhommière* would have been built as a summer residence by the landed gentry, hence the usual lack of outbuildings. They were usually built to conform with city fashions rather than the vernacular architecture of the area. All *gentilhommières* are built along the same plan of a central corridor leading to rooms on either side. Aside from these, there are all manner of old buildings crying out for restoration or renovation, ranging from simple barns to water mills, presbyteries, *chartreuses* (monasteries), disused factories and paper mills to old hospitals.

At the top of the scale, are the *châteaux* to be found throughout France. Originally built as defensive outposts in the Middle Ages, they gradually became more and more ornate, culminating in the splendid palaces built by the aristocracy when the French court was located along the Loire. After the French Revolution, *châteaux* were no longer the sole preserve of the aristocracy, but were built by wealthy landowners on a more modest scale. They are found throughout France in the most surprising places – one small *château* has even been reinvented as a car showroom in the centre of a roundabout. Some are small enough for the modern, nuclear family whereas others would be suitable for use as hotels or guesthouses. The larger *châteaux* are large enough to subdivide into self-contained apartments. If considering any of these options, don't underestimate the potential cost and time involved in the day-to-day running and upkeep of such a building.

If remote countryside does not appeal then one of France's 30,000 villages, or one of its small towns may seem preferable. The benefits of community life, local facilities and security suit many and are especially valuable if the property is to be rented out for part of the year. Old properties in small villages tend to be attached, with small windows to keep out the heat or the cold, depending on their location, so they are often rather dark inside. In medieval villages it is still possible to find original farmworker's houses complete with the large doors used for admitting machinery or animals.

Throughout France, houses are sold boasting original features, such as wooden or tiled floors, roof beams, doors and shutters, large open fireplaces, exposed stone walls, wooden staircases, bread ovens and cellars – the detail varying according to region. In the twentieth century, improved transport systems have blurred regional identities to some extent, but there are still visible distinctions. Grey or pink granite walls and dark slate roofs are abundant in Brittany; honey-coloured stone buildings predominate in the Dordogne; white limestone is common in the Loire; grey, volcanic stone buildings are often seen in the Auvergne. Where there was little stone to be quarried, then wood from the forests was used to build Alpine chalets, as well as the decorative *columbages* (half-timbered houses) of Normandy, Champagne, Picardy, the Landes and the Basque country. These timber-frames were filled in with wattle and daub or cob, and then rendered and painted. Alsace is particularly noted for its brightly painted half-timbered houses. Later, bricks and stone were used as infill – the fancier the decorative work, the wealthier the owner.

Home buyers are, of course, not restricted to old properties. Over recent years, greater interest has been shown in new buildings. On the coast, there are contemporary villas, apartments and studios to be explored, along with purpose-built complexes including facilities such as golf courses, tennis courts and restaurants. Because of demand from the French as well as foreign buyers, these properties are sold at premium prices, particularly if they have a sea view. There is also a growing trend for new buildings to be constructed in the style of the particular region. Using authentic or reclaimed local materials ensures that the property will blend with the local architecture, and has the advantage of providing modern conveniences in a traditional setting.

If thinking of setting up a business, why not consider taking over an existing concern, rather than starting from scratch. Establishing a popular *gîte*, for instance, will depend on its position, proximity to local attractions and coast or swimming pool. It may be less stressful to take over somewhere with an existing clientele. You don't have to be restricted to the *gîte* or *chambre d'hote* (B & B) businesses. For instance, vineyards need a lot of work and an experienced staff, but they do come onto the market. You could employ someone to manage one for you and simply sit back to enjoy the results.

how to find a property in France

Unless you are already living in France, the first thing to do is to acquaint yourself thoroughly with the sorts of properties available and the prices being asked for them. It is worth looking in the national newspapers, where both agents and private sales may be advertised. However, there are a number of magazines devoted to France and the French property market which may give you a better idea of what's around. *France, French Property News*, *Focus on France* and *Bonjour* are all specifically devoted to the country while *Homes Abroad*, *International Homes* and *Homes Overseas* cover French

Elaborate half-timbered houses line the narrow streets of Rennes.

property sales as well as those elsewhere. It is worth visiting the French property exhibitions that are held round the country to meet various agents (both French and English) and see the types of property they represent. Many French estate agents (*agents immobiliers*) operate through various UK-based agencies. In the event of using one, the commission is most usually split between the UK and French agents, costing the client nothing extra. If being sold a property at an 'all-in' price, it is wise to ask for a break-down of the costs so you can be sure that everything really is included, and that the UK agent is not charging a separate commission or consultancy fee in addition to the French fee.

There are various organizations of *agents immobiliers*, the most familiar being FNAIM (Fédération National des Agents Immobiliers) and SNPI (Syndicat National des Professionels Immobiliers). If you choose to deal directly with a French *agent immobilier* you will find that he is more strictly regulated than his British counterpart. He should have a *carte professionelle* from the local *préfecture* guaranteeing his professional competence, plus professional indemnity insurance, and occasionally he will have a financial guarantee allowing him to receive your deposit (although this is not the norm). You should ascertain the sum of the guarantee and the company covering it.

The agent should assist with the whole transaction, recommending, when necessary, professionals such as lawyers or building specialists whose advice you may need to seek. It is usual for the estate agent or *notaire*, not a solicitor, to prepare the *compromis de vente* (preliminary contract). If you have any doubts as to its contents, you may want to bring in your own lawyer for advice. There are a number of firms of solicitors in the UK who specialize in conveyancing in Europe or you may prefer to find an English-speaking lawyer in France through your estate agent or neighbouring ex-pats.

If you are in France, you may find a property through local papers, estate agents or through a *notaire*'s (notary's) office. A *notaire* is a government official legally responsible for overseeing and authenticating the transfer of title to a property, but he is also allowed to offer property for sale. Like an estate agent, his commission is fixed by law. Depending on where you are buying and whether you are buying from an estate agent or *notaire*, the agent's fees may be paid by the seller, the buyer, or split between them. If buying a house at auction (*vente aux enchères*), an appropriately registered *notaire* or lawyer must bid for you. These properties may have come onto the market because of inheritance disputes or defaults in mortgage repayments and can sometimes, though rarely, be bought at knock-down prices. Watch out for announcements in local papers.

How to buy a property in France

This is by necessity a brief and general guide. There is no substitute for professional legal advice regarding the individual requirements of each purchase.

The sale of property is strictly regulated in France and conducted by a *notaire* who represents neither the buyer nor the seller. If in any doubt about the procedures, it would be wise to find a solicitor who can explain them to you. Either ask your *agent immobilier* for a recommendation or engage one from a specialist firm in Britain. If you are buying a flat or a new property then there will be variations in the procedure that your lawyer should be able to explain to you.

The estate agent (or occasionally a *notaire*) will draw up a *compromis de vente*, which is a binding legal document recording the agreement to buy and sell between the vendor and the buyer. This document will include both parties' names, although it may be advisable to include a substitution clause so that another person or company can be inserted after questions of inheritance or taxation have been investigated thoroughly. The precise details of what is being sold should be spelled out. The purchase price, deposit and any additional fees will be mentioned. It will state that the vendor is not responsible for any defects in the property – so make sure you've done your homework. There will also be *conditions suspensives* (conditional clauses) which must be satisfied before the deal goes through. These will exempt you from going through with the purchase if, for example, you fail to obtain a mortgage, if the existing mortgage cannot be repaid from the sale, if you cannot obtain clear title to the property, if the boundaries are unclear or if there are building restrictions on the land. If any of these are not satisfied, then your deposit will be returned and the sale cancelled. If, on the other hand, a purchase fails through the buyer's fault, then he will forfeit the deposit. The contract also specifies a date for completion. After signing the *compromis*, there is a seven-day cooling-off period, during which the buyer can back out of the deal without any repercussions. Once this period is over, the buyer is committed to the purchase, provided all of its conditions are fulfilled. In some cases, a *promesse de vente* may be used instead of a *compromis*. This is an agreement in which the vendor sets out the details of the sale. Once the buyer agrees, the effect is the same as a *compromis*.

A deposit of 10 per cent is paid to the

Fields of red poppies brighten the Picardie landscape in spring.

The half-timbered (colombage) houses of Normandy are popular as comfortable second homes.

notaire (or, very occasionally, to the estate agent), who puts it into escrow (an independent third-party account) until completion. Remember, the buyer is responsible for paying both the legal costs and taxes relating to the purchase. If the property has been built within the last five years, the notary's fees will be between 2 and 3 per cent of the purchase price, whereas if it is older, you should expect his fees to be between 7 and 9 per cent. This covers you for stamp duty, land registry and conveyancing. There is nothing more to pay.

The *notaire* must conduct various searches and enquiries with the local authority and Land Charges Registry, but these relate to the property alone, not to its surroundings. It is up to you or your solicitor to conduct investigations into general planning proposals for the area, to discover whether a motorway is planned to run nearby, for example, or if a block of flats is to be built in the neighbouring field. When the *notaire* has completed his work he will draw up an *acte de vente* which, when signed, completes the transfer of property to the buyer. At this point, the balance of the money is due so the bank transfers need to have been arranged ahead.

The buyer is then issued with an *attestation*, a certificate proving that they are the owner of the property. The title deeds stay with the *notaire*, but a copy should be sent to the buyer within about three months. Land registry is proof of ownership.

planning permission

Buying an old property is not necessarily plain sailing. In the first instance, if the land exceeds a certain hectarage, neighbouring farmers may have to be given their right of first refusal. If planning on any major work, check at the local *mairie* (town hall) as to whether you will need permission for change of use or planning permission. If so, you will need a *Certificat d'Urbanisme*, similar to outline approval in the UK. This can be applied for from the *mairie* before the *compromis* (preliminary binding agreement) is signed and when granted will last for twelve months with the possibility of a further twelve-month extension. If the renovation is extensive then you (or your architect) will need to apply for a *permis de construire* (building permit) by submitting detailed plans to the *mairie* accompanied by a form they will provide for you to complete. Before signing a contract of sale, make enquiries to the *mairie* to see whether they are likely to have any objections in principal to your plans. In the French countryside, authorities will tend to take a *laissez-faire* attitude because they see the restoration of old buildings as beneficial to the local economy. You are unlikely to encounter many problems providing your proposals are in sympathy with the local architecture. Some towns and villages preserve their identity and sense of history by insisting on approval of any exterior work. They may even specify the paint colours for the woodwork. If your fantasies entail reclining by a pool, ensure permission will be granted for its construction. The same goes for the installation of a septic tank and for an alteration to the boundaries of a property. Also, make sure that you will have secure access to the property by car, and that the property can be connected to mains water and electricity. The local *mairie* should be able to answer all your questions.

grants

In exceptional circumstances, it may be possible to obtain a grant from the local council if you are restoring an old building, whether or not it is listed. If you are proposing to create a *gîte* from dilapidated farm buildings, the Gîtes de France may give you a grant. In return you will be tied to their organization for a number of years, and unable to let through any other. Before going down this route, make sure you understand the conditions of the grant and any effect they may have on the way you run your business. Another potential source of funding is the ANAH (*Agence National d'Amélioration d'Habitat*), which may contribute towards the improvement of a building that is more than fifteen years old, providing that it remains the owner's principal residence for at least nine years after the work is complete.

mortgages

If your finances do not run to a cash purchase, you may want to remortgage your home in the UK, borrowing against the equity, which will put you in the happy position of being a cash buyer. Alternatively, you could take out a mortgage with a French lender. But beware that there is an additional tax for the loan registration if a French lender is the source of your funds. You will be offered the choice of a fixed or variable rate, just the same as in the UK. Many UK banks and building societies have branches throughout France, or you may prefer to borrow from a French bank. You will need to provide them with details of your income and any financial obligations. It is important to shop around, comparing the relative interest rates, the length and nature of the repayment schemes and the percentage of the purchase price they are willing to lend. You should also decide whether it will be better to have a sterling or Euro mortgage. If in any doubt, seek the advice of an independent financial adviser or your lawyer. Remember that the mortgage only contributes to the cost of the property. The buyer must be able to cover the cost of the balance plus the additional conveyancing fees and property taxes.

insurance

The *notaire* will insist on seeing proof of insurance against third-party liability as soon as the buyer takes the title to the property. It is common to take over the insurance from the vendor. Having third-party liability insurance is a legal requirement, while taking the wholly sensible precaution of insuring your property against fire, flood, storm damage and the contents against theft is not. Shop around to make sure you buy insurance with a reputable and reliable company that is financially stable. Read the small print in your agreement carefully, so you know exactly what you are covered for. If yours is a holiday home, you will need a special holiday home policy that will cover you if you are away from the property for long periods.

inheritance law

French law governs French property whether or not the owner is a resident in the country and this also applies to how your property is passed on within your family. Unlike English law, French law does not allow you to choose the beneficiaries of your will. The Napoleonic Code gives priority to the children of the deceased. The children have an automatic right to a fixed interest in the property, the remaining part to be allocated at will. This includes the children of former marriages or those who are estranged. If there are no children, then the parents of the deceased automatically receive a reserved portion. There are, however, ways of avoiding French succession law. Probably the most common is to include a *clause tontine* in the contract at the time of purchase. Sometimes referred to as a 'wait and see' clause, it means that ownership of the entire property is effectively

A typical high house with distinctively shaped tiled roofs from Sarlat in the Dordogne.

suspended until one of the couple dies. At that point, the surviving spouse becomes the owner. Alternatively, it is possible to buy through a French property-holding company (*société civilé immobilière* or SCI) whereby a husband and wife hold shares in the company. As long as they are not French residents, the shares will not be subject to French inheritance laws. Tax implications make it wise to take UK tax advice before going down this route. Another alternative is for the property to be bought through an offshore company or trust. Both of these are less frequently recommended because of the potentially high tax liabilities. Always seek sound legal advice from the start of your negotiations to avoid unforeseen ramifications. It is not possible to change the legal structure once the purchase has been made without incurring full registration fees again (9 per cent). All immoveable property in France is subject to French law on the owner's death. There are three types of will that can be drawn up: holographic – handwritten, unwitnessed and can be filed in the central wills registry; notarial – dictated, witnessed and automatically filed in the central wills registry; secret – sealed in an envelope before being given to the *notaire*. A holographic will is the most commonly used but you should take legal advice to make sure you have covered all eventualities.

Living in France

residency

EU citizens are entitled to live anywhere within the European Union. But if planning to become a permanent resident in France, you will need to apply for a *carte de séjour* from the local *préfecture*. Each *préfecture* differs slightly on which documents need to be provided. If you are not earning a living, for example, you are a pensioner or a student, you may be asked to produce proof of financial support. If you are not of pensionable age you will need to produce proof of health insurance.

work

EU citizens do not need a work permit to work in a member country. However, there are some professions that demand a French qualification.

social security

France operates a social security system similar to that in the UK. Registration is obligatory if you are employed. Your employer will register you, and you will be issued with a social insurance card. The social security system is financed by employer/employee contributions. It covers a portion of the risks or expenses of illness, disability, old age, death, maternity, work accidents and family benefits. Consult leaflet SA29 from the DSS for details of social security, pension rights and healthcare within the EU.

pensions

If retiring to France, it is a wise precaution to take some pension planning advice. Pensioners are entitled to receive their UK state pension, receiving the annual increases and Christmas bonus. If you are a French resident, then you must declare any private pension as part of your worldwide income and pay French tax on it. If you have already paid UK tax on it, you can claim to have it refunded.

bank account

If you are taking out a French mortgage, it is necessary to open a French bank account, for which you will need proof of your address and your identity. It is possible to open either a non-resident's or a resident's account, but it's worth noting that non-residents, while they may obtain mortgages or car loans, are not allowed overdrafts. With your cheque account comes a *carte bleue* which is similar to a Switch card and can be used in cash machines or to pay in shops, restaurants, cinemas and garages. If you do allow yourself to become overdrawn and are unable to put yourself back within your limit within a month of receiving a warning letter, your account will be automatically closed and your name will be listed as unsuitable to open a bank account for one year. Even if you do not need to open a French bank account for a mortgage, having one does make paying your French bills much more straightforward.

government

France is a republic governed by a president elected every seven years by public vote. The French parliament is composed of a Senate and National Assembly which is responsible for nominating a Prime Minister to be appointed by the President to run the government. Metropolitan France is divided into 22 regions subdivided into 96 departments, which in turn are divided into communes governed by a mayor elected by a municipal council. The mayor provides the crucial link between the people of France and the government. It is the *mairie* (town hall) that will be crucial to any foreigner moving into the area, which will be able to provide answers to any planning question as well as to regulations that may affect them.

furniture and goods

For an EU citizen there are no restrictions on taking personal property and household goods into France. If you are moving antiques, make sure you have a certificate proving that they originate in the UK, otherwise moving them back to the UK may be problematic.

taxes

What follows is by necessity a very simplified account. It is sensible to seek professional advice to find a path through the maze of financial planning.

INCOME TAX: The first distinction to make is whether or not you are a French resident. You are considered to be a resident if you spend more than 183 days a year in France, or if your permanent home is in France (even if you spend less than 183 days there), or if you are not a tax resident anywhere else but have accommodation in France and visit the country regularly (even for less than 183 days).

RESIDENT: If you become a French resident, you will be liable to French taxes on all your worldwide assets and income. When leaving the UK, you should submit a P85 to your tax inspector, stating your residence intentions. Employees must usually submit their own tax returns in the same way as self-employed people do. The financial year runs from 1 January to 31 December. If your return is filed later than the end of February, you will incur a 10 per cent penalty. Most people choose to pay their taxes in three instalments, but it as possible to arrange payment in ten monthly instalments. There are local tax offices that can guide you through the form and its complications, or you may prefer to use an independent tax accountant.

NON-RESIDENT: If you are a non-resident of France, you are liable to pay tax on any rent you receive from letting your property, even if you receive the money in the UK. The rate will depend on whether or not the house is furnished or unfurnished and whether you own it yourself or through a company (see above). However, because of the double tax treaty between the UK and France, whatever you pay in France will be offset against your UK tax assessment.

PROPERTY TAX: Additional costs to the house owner come in the form of two taxes that are equivalent to the UK's council tax. The *taxe d'habitation* is paid by the occupant of the house and is based on the notional letting value of the property according to the Land Registry. The *impôt foncier* is the land tax, payable by the owner on a property whether inhabited or not. New houses may be exempt from this, as are derelict properties until they have been restored. Apply to the local tax office if you are unsure. Both these are collected annually in arrears.

CAPITAL GAINS TAX: Capital gains tax is payable on the profit made from selling property in France if it is a second home, the amount depending on the amount of time it has been owned. Double tax relief is available. Property owned for over twenty-two years is exempt from CGT. Remember to keep all TVA (VAT) receipts resulting from the original purchase as well as from any building or renovation work. Eventually you may be able to offset them against CGT. The tax rate for non-residents is 33 per cent.

INHERITANCE TAX: Inheritance tax is payable by the heirs to a will, irrespective of whether or not they live in France. The rate is variable and depends on the value of the assets they inherit and the relationship of the heirs to the deceased. The tax will be alleviated if the deceased had taken out life assurance. In the case of a deceased French resident, inheritance tax is payable on all assets, wherever they may be. The tax is payable by the spouse and heirs of the deceased. The same applies to gift tax but reductions are made depending on the age of the heir: the younger they are, the greater the reduction.

VAT: The current standard rate is 19.6 per cent.

education

If you are moving to France with a young family, your children's education will be one of the key factors determining where you choose to live. Until the age of about nine or ten, children will pick up a new language surprisingly quickly and will settle into local schools without too many problems.

The French education system is renowned for its thorough, traditionalist approach. All children between the ages of three to five are eligible for *l'école maternelle*, or nursery school. Since 1967, primary and then secondary schooling has been obligatory for all six to sixteen-year-olds. Primary school operates in two stages: the first three years cover the CP (*cours préparatoire)* and CE1 and CE2 (*cours élémentaire)* to provide a grounding in basic skills which include French, maths, science, history and geography; the fourth and fifth year cover the CM1 and CM2 (*cours moyen)*, during which a foreign language may be introduced. At this level, many schools do not have classes on Wednesdays, but have school on Saturday morning instead. Secondary education begins at age eleven, with entry to a *Collège* or Junior Secondary School. In classes six (*sixième*) to thirteen (*troisième*) enormous importance is placed on maths and sciences, and one or two foreign languages will be introduced. At thirteen, a pupil can opt to follow a general education course or a course with a vocational bias. The final two years of school are taught at a *Lycée* or High School, where the curriculum is continued, with an added emphasis on personal study. In the final year, students either sit for one of various vocational qualifications or for the *Baccalauréat (le Bac)*. These examinations will determine whether a student goes on to technical or vocational colleges, or university. If they do particularly well, they become eligible to sit the entrance exams for the *Grandes Ecoles*, which are the top French universities.

If your children are already at secondary stage and speak only limited French, it might be counter-productive to throw them headlong into this system. A better solution might be found in larger towns, where some of the state schools run international sections, catering for bilingual and foreign students. Alternatively, you may prefer one of the private fee-paying schools that are usually international and either follow the education system of their own country or the International *Baccalauréat*.

When choosing a solution that best suits your family, think about where your child will benefit most both socially and academically. Being able to make local friends and mix with the community rather than being schooled in a more isolating environment may make all the difference to their happiness.

healthcare

The French health service is held up as a shining example of its kind. Unlike the UK system, you can choose which doctor or specialist you prefer to visit. If you are becoming a permanent resident, do remember to take your medical records to France when you move, so that they can be referred to if necessary. The system is simple. EU nationals must apply for a social security number. You pay for your treatment or prescription, and then complete a form signed by the doctor to allow you

The houses of the bastide town of Domme are built of the honey-coloured stone so typical of the Dordogne.

pets

Provided your pets have an up-to-date Anti-Rabies Vaccination certificate, they will be allowed to enter France without a quarantine period. They will not be allowed back into the UK without a pet passport and microchip.

cars

If taking your car to France permanently, you may be charged tax if it is under six months old or has less than a 6,000 km mileage. If you take your car to France for longer than six months, its registration will have to be changed at the *préfecture*. Cars over five years old must undergo a *contrôle technique* (MOT). The tax disc is renewable annually in November. British nationals can drive on their British licence.

to claim a fixed percentage of the cost back. Before making an appointment, check whether or not they are *médecins conventionnés secteur un*. If they are, their fees will fall within the limits set by the health service, and you will be reimbursed accordingly. Other doctors (*médecins conventionnés secteur deux* or *médecins non conventionées*) may charge more, so you will need some form of insurance to pay the difference between the cost of the treatment and the amount reimbursed by social security. If you want to be refunded 100 per cent, then you will need to take out private medical insurance to cover the difference. If you are already insured by a British company, check whether their policy will cover you in France. Families covered by social security may have a green *carte vitale*, which should be taken to the doctor on every visit. This will transfer all the necessary information between the doctor and social services and does away with the need for any form.

An E106 (from the DSS) gives British nationals reciprocal health cover for two years after a move abroad. The amount of cover granted depends on the amount of National Insurance you have paid in the previous three years. If you are neither resident nor employed in France and wish to make a claim, then you should send an E111 (available from all English post offices) off with the claim and any relevant receipts. If you are a resident with a pension from the UK you need to provide your local French Health Insurance Centre with an E121 (from DSS), the receipt for your application for residence, your birth certificate and a French bank or post office identification slip. You will then be reimbursed a percentage of the cost of your treatment.

mains services

ELECTRICITY: Before moving in to your new home, you or your estate agent should contact the EDF (*Electricité de France*) to notify them, to ask them to read the meter and to then change the account to your name. You will be liable to pay a connection charge and, if a non-resident, possibly a deposit. If electricity has to be installed in an old property, the EDF will quote a charge for extending it from the nearest point. The charge may by prohibitive depending on the scale of the work, so check it before buying the property.

GAS: Mains gas is not yet generally provided to rural areas, where cylinder gas is the norm. If in a town or city, application must be made to the GDF (Gaz de France) in the same way as to the EDF (above).

WATER: Mains water doesn't come cheap in France and is supplied by various private companies. Apply to your local company to connect you, after reading the meter before you move in. If moving to a property without mains water, apply to the local company for a quotation for laying pipes and installing a meter.

House hunters

Aude
Paul Bennett and Deena Harris

Builder Paul Bennett, his partner Deena Harris and their six-year-old daughter, Sydney, had decided to sell up and move abroad. Sick of the English weather, despairing at the price of land and yearning for the good life, they followed their hearts to France where they'd often holidayed. They were looking for a major project to work on by themselves. 'We wanted something that needed total renovation that we could put something of ourselves in.' They had already spent a year looking in the south but this time they were determined not to go home empty-handed. They came armed with a budget of £80,000 for the property and another £80,000 for the necessary work.

The first property they saw was an unconverted farmhouse in the lush, rolling foothills of the **PYRENEES**, where there is a rich tapestry of wheat, maize, soya and sunflower fields, not forgetting the herds of dairy cows. Here, the mountains are peppered with fortified castles, the last dramatic vestiges of the Cathars. Many old farmhouses have been converted in the region but they found one that was as derelict as they were hoping to find. For £30,000, there was a two-storey barn in two and a half acres with electricity, water and a roof. 'This is very much what we're looking for. It's got the beams, the stone and it's in a fantastic location.' It certainly presented a completely blank canvas. The owner was thinking of splitting the land and only selling just over an acre with the barn, in which case Paul and Deena were advised to ensure that the boundaries to the property were set out clearly in the contract. However, they decided not to make an offer anyway because they wanted to hold out for a detached property.

Above: Paul Bennett and Deena Harris view an unconverted farmhouse with presenter Amanda Lamb.

Below: A fourteenth-century presbytery in a remote village in Carcassone offered scope for renovation.

The next location was a small village just outside **CARCASSONE**, the third most popular tourist destination in France. At £91,000, this fourteenth-century presbytery was over Paul and Deena's budget, but offered huge potential and a number of local facilities, most crucially a school for their daughter and free transport to and from it. Once the home of the local priest, it had more recently been used as a family home. The property offered a huge attic, three double bedrooms, a small but well-equipped kitchen, a vast, open-plan living/dining area leading to the kitchen and breakfast bar. Although it didn't have a garden, there

Above: A two-bedroom mansion originally built for a wine-grower looked deceptively small from the outside.

Below: Restoring a barn on the outskirts of Mirepoix was exactly the sort of project Paul and Deena had in mind.

was a shady south-facing terrace ideal for outdoor eating. 'There was a superb, typically French, windy road to the lovely remote village. It feels like it's on top of the world.' The building was crying out to be renovated but, not having any land, it wasn't quite what they wanted.

Their search took them to the village of **VILLELONGUE** in the heart of the wine-growing area where most of the 187 inhabitants are still involved in wine production. Living here would give Paul and Deena all the benefits of living in a remote but friendly community. There was a two-bedroom mansion, flat-fronted with a central wrought-iron balcony, that had been built for a wealthy local producer. It had two, airy reception rooms and a shell of a kitchen. Upstairs, the bathroom needed remodelling and had only been partially walled off while above that there was a partially renovated attic. Next door was a vast two-storey barn complete with vats where wine had once been stored. 'Our first thought was that it was a definite no-no. But it opened up like the Tardis inside.' But Paul felt the work that had already been done was unreliable and would have to be ripped out. Otherwise, they both loved the original floor tiles and fireplaces and felt it would have great potential. It had the added bonus of having a nearby school in the village for Sydney. The house was for sale at £69,000 with the barn at £22,000. Paul and Deena could see the possibilities but ultimately he felt 'there was too much bodging' so they decided to look elsewhere.

The medieval *bastide* town of **MIREPOIX** was built round a beautiful market square with rare, covered arcades. On its outskirts a large working farm offered a barn for sale at £60,000. It had two floors, a splendid timber roof, a couple of pigs and an astonishing fifty acres of land. In 1944, the Germans had burned the original building to the ground when they discovered resistance fighters hiding there. It had been rebuilt six years later by the French government. Paul and Deena were ecstatic. 'It has great character, is in a perfect setting in a peaceful valley. Exactly what we're looking for.' They were advised to ensure that the boundaries were included in the contract, not forgetting to make the clearance of all the rubbish and machinery a condition of sale. Although they wanted enough land to ensure their privacy, they acknowledged that fifty acres was too much. They decided to offer £40,000 for the barn and the two and a half acres in front of it. However, the agent told them a similar offer had already been refused.

Eventually, they went to the **LOT**, an area they knew well. They were drawn by the architecture, the weather and its remoteness plus the added bonus of a friend who had already moved there. Finally, they found their ideal property by chance when they noticed an *A Vendre* sign on a wall. There was a dilapidated house with a

Left and below: An uninhabitable house in the Lot had the potential the couple were looking for.

pigeonnière, flanked by a bread oven on one side, a barn on the other – all completely uninhabitable. They chatted with the owner on site and the next day they put down their deposit with the *notaire* in order to buy the property for just under £40,000. Just before Christmas, 2001, they towed a five-berth caravan, their temporary living quarters, to their new property and began the restoration work. By February, the EDF had connected a new electricity supply and Paul, a qualified electrician, was planning to rewire the property using English fittings to suit all their appliances. When finished, the house will comprise two living rooms, four bedrooms (the master bedroom and ensuite in the main house, Sydney's backing into the *pigeonnière*, and one on each of the first and second storeys of the barn), a large kitchen/dining room, an office, a downstairs shower and washroom, a gym and storage area in the basement, a double garage and car workshop on the ground floor of the barn and a second workshop below. The property came with half an acre of land but they plan to buy a further six acres. They have been told that agricultural land can only be sold in plots of less than 2,499 square metres if it is not to be offered to neighbouring landowners, so their smallholding will accumulate gradually.

Having opened an account at the local builder's merchant, Paul is the building foreman with Deena as his labourer (for a good wage!). They plan completion within two years by which time they hope to have been absorbed into the local community. 'We want to fit in and live the local lifestyle in a house built in the style and manner of the region. Already the residents of our small hamlet have made us all feel very welcome and have invited us to wine and dine at their houses. We're going to disappear from our old existence and enjoy our life as a family here.' Sydney will go to the local school by school bus, once permission is formally granted by the local mayor. Paul and Deena plan to enjoy the next two years' work not as work but more as a huge hobby, enjoying the quality of their new life.

House hunters

Brittany
Lesley Cooper and Stuart Robinson

Once you've got the bug for France, it's hard to shake off, as two members of the police force, Lesley Cooper and Stuart Robinson, found out. They had decided to look for a second home in Brittany. They had researched the area on the Net, liking its resemblance to Cornwall, its reasonable property prices and its accessibility from Yorkshire, bearing in mind that their two dogs would be coming along.

An independent duchy until 1532, Brittany occupies the north-western tip of France. The Bretons have retained their spirit of individualism to this day. Local fare of crêpes and cider, traditional costumes and music, and even the ancient Breton language of Breiz are all still to be found here, particularly in the west. The coastline offers impressive beaches in the north, a rocky west-facing shore swept by Atlantic winds and a milder, wooded southern side. Inland Brittany is known as Argoat, 'the wooded country', where the landscape is immersed in myth and legend, dotted with ruined castles, magical forests and standing stones. Small fishing villages and port towns are strung along the coast, while inland there are well-preserved towns of historical interest such as Fougères, Vitré and Comburg. The capital, the university town of Rennes, is particularly noted for the half-timbered houses remaining in its old quarter. Tourism is mostly concentrated on the coast, while quiet and relaxation can readily be found only a short drive inland. There are numerous walking and cycling trails, quiet canals, rivers and lakes, thirty-two golf courses, and a number of nature reserves to satisfy bird watchers. Thanks to the Gulf Stream, the climate is similar to that of Cornwall and milder than much of the rest of northern France.

The original features retained in this picturesque granite cottage in Morbihan gave it plenty of character.

Leslie and Stuart were looking for a two- to three-bedroom house, typically Breton in style, with a small garden. They had a budget of £40,000. The first property they saw was in the unspoilt wooded landscape of **MORBIHAN**, on the south coast. The Gulf of Morbihan is almost enclosed by land and is an internationally renowned bird sanctuary. There are fine sandy beaches, a rolling green landscape with plenty of unspoilt historic buildings. Here they found a two-bedroom, granite cottage with a characteristic slate roof, a garden and a separate plot of land for £22,000. Inside, there was a light, spacious living area with some exposed stonework on the walls, ceiling beams and a large Breton fireplace, a good sized kitchen, a master bedroom and an attic bedroom. It was everything they'd imagined: cosy, romantic, 'almost chocolate box'. The separate plot was ideal for a mobile home or a pool if planning permission could be obtained from the mayor. With the estate agent's fees included in the asking price, it represented fantastic value for money. 'We immediately fell in love with the property on walking through the door. It felt like home.'

The economy of Brittany has largely depended on the sea, so the coastal towns supported the trades of fishing, ship-building, piracy and smuggling. In the village of **LOQUIREC** on the Côte d'Armor was a restored two-bedroom house with a covered porch, garden and terrace. Inside there was a huge, light living room, a modern kitchen and a bathroom characteristically lined with teak. It looked traditional from the outside, but the inside, though beautiful, was too modern for Stuart and Lesley. It was over their budget and they were agreed that it was 'private, pristine but pricey.' To cover the cost of going over their budget, they would be able to consider renting the house when they weren't using it and could expect to get £300–£400 per week in rental. However, this wasn't enough to sway them.

Above: A traditional exterior hid the modern interior of this two-bedroom cottage in Loquirec.
Below: The attention paid to detail in the renovation of a farmhouse in the Morbihan areas was impressive.

The third property they saw was deep in the **MORBIHAN** countryside. The concentration of menhirs, dolmens and other standing stones make it one of the most important megalithic sites in the world. It's a sparsely populated agricultural area with fields of maize, wheat and cows. Many of the properties here are sold to be second homes, so Stuart and Lesley were pleased to view an idyllic, three-bedroom farmhouse with a stable and barn sitting in two and a half acres of land. It had various original features, among them exposed stone walls and ceiling beams. 'It took our breath away. It's big, nicely done up with a high standard of workmanship. It's also got a number of business possibilities we might investigate.' The couple couldn't afford to move there permanently, but the letting potential would perhaps make it a feasible buy. They could rent the main house out for £350 a week and there was the possibility of creating a *gîte* from the barn that would bring in £200 a week. Lesley was also attracted by the future possibility of being able to keep a horse there.

Finally, they went to **ROCHEFORT-EN-TERRE**, a delightful half-timbered medieval town built by wealthy noblemen who were guillotined during the French Revolution. During the nineteenth century, it was home to an artist's colony and to this day it has retained its bohemian feel. In a nearby village, a fully furnished, two-bedroom *longère* (longhouse) was for sale, complete with a plum, apricot and apple orchard. This was an ideal holiday cottage, which they would be able to move into immediately. It was in a picturesque location, had a good-sized garden and a loft space that could be converted into a large living area – all for £27,000. The catch was that it was situated in a flood zone, which had been flooded six times since 1996. This particular house had been under a foot of water at least once. That news put Lesley and Stuart off going any further.

In the end, Stuart and Leslie were so torn between the renovated farmhouse and the stone cottage in Morbihan, that they decided to put in an offer in on both

Above: Despite the undoubted attractions of this longère, *it had the major disadvantage of being located on a flood plain.*

and see what happened. Both offers were turned down, but, undaunted, they decided to try again. The owner of the Morbihan farmhouse wouldn't drop the price, so they focussed on the cottage and offered £20,000. To their delight it was accepted. 'We were a bit apprehensive because we speak little French and were venturing into the unknown.' They didn't use a solicitor even though translating the *compromis de vente* with the help of a dictionary was 'a nightmare'. Eventually, they found a friend who could help them, bought a fax machine and faxed it back to France. 'We went in there totally blind, but just decided to take it full on ourselves.' When they went to France to sign it officially, a second *compromis* had to be drawn up because they'd somehow messed up the first one (to this day, they are not sure how). Their seven-day cooling off period eventually took place two months after they had made the offer. They feel the best thing they did was join Oui Can Help, an organization that helped them sort out what the estate agent needed, made their appointments with the *notaire*, organized the water and electricity connections, and so on. After four months, the *acte de vente* was signed. They employed David Moody, a builder, to knock through the back part of the cottage to make a new kitchen, lay a concrete floor, put on a new roof with velux windows and install a water-heating

system. Finally, Lesley and Stuart were able to go out and start work of their own. After their first freezing winter night there, the fireplace was swiftly replaced with an efficient wood-burning stove. A qualified electrician, Stuart was able to rewire the place, and, with a tiling course under his belt, he tiled the kitchen floor before insulating the roof and adding a new kitchen door. They've been welcomed into the area by neighbouring English ex-pats and, as their French improves, they're hoping to integrate into the local community too. In fact, now that the dogs have passports, they're already dreaming about retiring there.

Above and right: Buying this house was just the beginning of the story. Lesley and Stuart immediately began work on their new kitchen.

House hunters

Normandy
Emma and Geoff Sallows

Like Brittany, Normandy is just a hop across the channel making a convenient location for a second home especially for those living in southern England. Emma and Geoff Sallows had dreamed of buying a beautiful, English country house but realized that they could get better value for their money by buying in France. Long-time Francophiles, they appreciate everything from the people and the pace of life to the food and wine. The possibility of owning a property there presented itself to them as a great adventure.

Normandy enjoys fertile green countryside divided by hedges and trees ('bocage') which inspired the Impressionist school of painters. It is a place of apple orchards, dairy farms, half-timbered houses in medieval villages and a coast notable for the D-Day landings. Only a couple of hours' train ride from Paris, the elegant coastal resorts, among them Honfleur, Deauville and Trouville, are popular with holidaying Parisians and are consequently quite pricey. The region is noted for its rich dairy produce, particularly the Camembert, and its cider and Calvados. Attractions include the D-Day beaches and cemeteries, the Abbey of Mont St Michel, the remarkable Bayeux tapestry and Monet's house at Giverny.

Above: Presenter Amanda Lamb with Geoff and Emma Sallows in Normandy.
Below: A typical Normandy house well-situated on the outskirts of Orbec.

Emma and Geoff were looking for an 'older-style property with a large garden surrounded by lovely countryside' to fall within their budget of £45,000. 'We'd like a beautiful interior complete with original beams and wood floors – the sort of thing we could never afford in England.' They had looked in Normandy before this trip and had decided that, with their two young sons, Finley and Brodie, they wanted to be close to the coast. This time, their first port of call was in the Pays d'Auge where the green fields and wooded valleys dotted with dairy farms are reminiscent of southern England. The picturesque town of **ORBEC** is dominated by a Norman church and is characterized by its many half-timbered houses. Just outside the town was a typical, three-bedroom Normandy house on the market for £41,000. It offered a living/dining room, a kitchen, bathroom, office, garage and a small, established garden. The cosy living/dining room was long and heavily beamed with a compact tiled kitchen just off it. Upstairs, the master bedroom was larger than they'd expected, despite its position in the

attic space. Spacious and well-situated, it offered the best of both town and country life. 'It was really perfect. We loved everything about it – the location, house and garden.' Their only caveat was the trees that blocked the view. Although the main part of the house was a hundred years old, the extension and garage had been added more recently and so, before buying, the Sallows would have to check they had been built with planning permission, as well as getting an expert to check for woodworm and damp in the beams. Ultimately, they decided they didn't have enough capital to do the necessary work.

Next, they ventured into the gentle hills surrounding the village of **SAINTE VIGOR DES MONTS**. Normandy

Above: The farmhouse outside Sainte Vigor des Monts had plenty of potential but, with two small children, there was too much work to be done. Below: A pine chalet on a complex near Deauville offered great facilities for the children.

produces over 2,000 varieties of apple, and Sainte Vigor is right in the heart of apple country. Just outside the sleepy village was a nineteenth-century, two-bedroom farmhouse, commanding spectacular views from its hilltop position. A working farm until recently, it had a vegetable garden, a hay barn, other outbuildings and two and a half acres of land. The interior was dated and the original character of the living room had been lost, although the original beams and fireplace could be restored. The primitive bathroom would have to be thoroughly renovated. There was no question that the property had bags of potential, but at £49,000 was well over the Sallows' budget. The outbuildings could be converted into *gîtes*, or alternatively they could be sold off with a bit of land for around £7,000 each. Tempting as it was, Emma and Geoff felt that now that they had children, there would be too much work involved.

Next on their route was the up-market resort town of **DEAUVILLE**. Central to the world of French horse-racing, it has its own airport, a casino (a favourite with Churchill) and an annual film festival. The town itself boasts a long sandy beach and promenade with quieter beaches close by along the coast. Outside the town, a holiday complex was offering nineteen chalets for sale. For £28,000, Emma and Geoff could own a two-bedroom pine chalet with a compact but functional kitchen, an attic mezzanine which could be used as living space or extra bedroom, a living/dining area, a deck terrace and small garden. Only ten minutes from the sea, it was a surprisingly spacious home in a safe, child-friendly environment. The family would also have use of the communal pool, the playground and mini-golf course. 'The different colours of the chalets made the atmosphere fun and exciting. We were pleasantly surprised although it's a long way from our original thoughts of a traditional old house or cottage.' The complex was extremely popular and the management had plans for tennis courts, riding stables and an overhaul of the mini-golf course all in hand. The additional annual maintenance charge of £1,800 could be recouped by renting the chalet for around £500 during the high season.

Before finally making up their minds, Emma and Geoff travelled to the Contentin peninsula to look at one last property. Surrounded on three sides by the Channel, the landscape is more wild and windy than the rest of the region but the west coast benefits from the Gulf Stream and is a popular summer retreat. Close to the village of **St Pierre de Servilly**, was a picturesque, one-bedroom stone cottage being sold privately for £44,000. Inside, the living area had bright red walls and was divided to provide a spare sleeping area, an office area and sitting space with a small kitchen and a tranquil white bedroom. A ladder led up the outside of the house to the attic with potential for conversion into a couple of bedrooms and bathroom. A local builder estimated that to add a spiral staircase and convert the attic

would cost £3,500. The house was peaceful and secluded and the Sallows loved everything about it, 'We loved the setting, the big warm living room and the potential offered by the attic space'. This charming cottage in its countryside setting won their hearts. They decided to go back home and work out their finances before making an offer of £44,000, which would include some of the furniture. When their offer was accepted, Emma and Geoff did all the negotiations from the UK. Appointing a large and well-known English firm of solicitors did have disadvantages. In retrospect they think they would have been better off with a smaller firm, who might have given them more attention throughout the purchase. As it was, they were passed from partner to partner, receiving conflicting advice. They were told too late that paying in sterling directly to the owner meant that the property would be uninsured for the period between sending the money and signing the contract because the fee would have to be exchanged into francs for the *notaire*. It also cost an additional £1,500 because the owner had agreed a fixed exchange rate. Instead of going to France to sign the *acte de vente*, they appointed a French-speaking solicitor in Brighton who acted for them. At last, they were able to visit their property for the first time, driving two cars there carrying everything they needed – including the children! 'It was freezing cold in December but we're looking forward to going there six times a year and renting it in between.' They found a local couple through *French Property News* who can look after day-to-day maintenance and change-over days, and who has already begun to provide invaluable advice and information, not to mention peace of mind. Emma plans to look after the rental calendar herself. The Sallows' great adventure is only just beginning.

Above and below: This one-bedroom cottage near St Pierre de Servilly provided all the answers to the Sallows' househunting requirements.

House hunters

Auvergne
Peter and Sharon Casley

Peter and Sharon Casley come from Derbyshire where Peter, otherwise known as the 'Big Cheese', owns a company manufacturing cheese-making machines, and Sharon is the company secretary. Peter and Sharon were looking for something 'olde worlde' with terrific views that fell within their budget of £90,000. They planned to use the property as a holiday home until Peter's retirement when they would move permanently. They had frequently holidayed in France but the region of Auvergne was new to them. Pockmarked with extinct volcanoes in the west, with the mountainous regions of Livradois, Forez and Velay to the east, its dramatic landscape offers a host of activities from summer water sports on the many lakes and rivers to winter skiing in the mountains. The region is dotted with Romanesque churches, *châteaux* and medieval castles. There are ten spa towns, including Vichy, Bourbon-l'Archambault and Châtel-Guyon, Thiers, the cutlery capital, and Clermont Ferrand, the commercial centre of this predominantly rural region.

ARLANC is a typical French town in the heart of the Parc Naturel Régional Livradois-Forez. Its winding streets, twelfth-century church and weekly local market add to its distinctive character. There's a strong tradition of lace-making in the region and Arlanc boasts the largest lace museum in France. Just outside the town, Peter and Sharon viewed a hundred-year-old, three-bedroom traditional farmhouse on the market for £61,000. It consisted of two bathrooms, a small kitchen, living room, study, a large cellar and attic with an outhouse and barn, ideal for converting into *gîtes*. It retained many original features, including ceiling beams and tiled floors and had great potential for renovation. Peter and Sharon loved it. 'It's amazing: so much bigger than it looks from the outside – and such beautiful views. I can just see us sitting there in front of a roaring log fire with a glass of wine in the winter.' They considered the possibility of converting the enormous attic space into a *gîte* too. If they wanted to add new windows, make any other external alterations to the building or add a pool in the garden, they would need planning permission. It was estimated that a pool would cost £10,000 per forty square metres. However, the cost would eventually be covered by the additional rent they would be able to charge for the *gîtes*. Peter's only other concern was the public footpath that ran between the garden and the house, but all things considered, it seemed a minor inconvenience.

Sensibly, they wanted to look at other properties in the region before coming to any decision. Their next stop was in the **LIVRADOIS-FOREZ PARK**, a protected area filled with lakes and crossed with waterways. It is home

Just outside Arlanc, a farmhouse offered all the potential the Casleys needed, as well as the opportunity of converting the outbuildings into gîtes.

to the water-based industries of paper-making and knife production. Aside from this, there are wonderful opportunities here for riding, hiking and water sports. To Peter and Sharon's surprise, they were able to see a twelfth-century *château* that fell within their budget. Behind the original façade and tower were five bedrooms, two bathrooms, three reception rooms, a chapel, and a dilapidated east wing with potential for future expansion. Outside, there was a walled garden and an east-facing terrace. The previous owner had considered using the property as a conference centre, but Peter and Sharon felt there would be more mileage in using the *château* as a hotel and converting the east

wing into a home for themselves. But for that price, there had to be a catch – it was only 200 yards from a busy motorway. However, Peter and Sharon were undaunted. What better way to bring customers straight to their door? In the end, they reluctantly decided that although it was a dream home, ultimately it was too big for them and needed too much work.

Above: A small château could provide a slice of gracious living in the Livradois National Park. Below left and right: A house built into the original city wall in the medieval village of Mareugheol would make an idiosyncratic home.

The medieval village of **MAREUGHEOL** lies in the volcanic foothills. Many of the villages in the area were once *bastide* villages with protecting, fortified walls. A three-bedroom house and an adjacent *gîte* occupied a corner of the original wall and were on the market together for £81,500. The unusual interior reflected the exterior with the kitchen and bathroom fitted into a corner tower. There was a spacious living room, complete with large fireplace, which led into a small study and a large, bright master bedroom which retained many original features. The next-door *gîte* slept four and opened onto the largest of the three terraces belonging to the property. 'Quaint and beautifully decorated' was their verdict on the inside. It was the outside that presented the problems. Peter and Sarah enjoy gardening and eating outdoors. The only way to reach the big terrace was to walk all the way around the house and, because Mareugheol is a listed village with strict building regulations, there was no question of being able to build an external staircase from the house directly to the terrace. The fact there was no garden was the final deciding factor against it.

CLERMONT FERRAND is a busy, university town and commercial centre where the Michelin brothers established their tyre business in 1886. The old town is built on

Above left and right: The rockface dictated the shape of the rooms in this unusual house.

the site of a defunct volcano, its buildings, including the dramatic Gothic cathedral, using stones hewn from the volcanic rock. Just outside the town, an old four-bedroom farmhouse was for sale in a village where all the houses were built into the rock face. The asking price was £73,500. It was completely different from the other properties they'd viewed, with the rock walls dictating the shape of the rooms and lending a distinctly cavernous atmosphere to the place. There was even a spectacular indoor swimming pool. Sadly, the property had been let go over the previous ten years and was in need of considerable attention. A local builder suggested enlarging the small kitchen by knocking it through into a small adjoining bedroom, turning a vast pottery studio on the top floor into a master bedroom and ensuite bathroom, and then opening up the downstairs and adding another bathroom. He gave an estimate for the work of £25,000. But Peter was adamant. He'd banged his head on the ceilings three times already, and anyway he felt the place was more suitable as a bachelor pad than a family home.

Tempted by the farmhouse in Arlanc, they were shocked on their return home to find the asking price had been hiked up another £6-7000. They were more pleasurably shocked to find that Sharon was pregnant, meaning that their plans have had to change. Sharon feels that the pleasures of travelling that distance with a baby in the back of the car will be short-lived, so wants to look again nearer one of the ferry ports. Her heart is set on Brittany or Normandy, though Peter yearns for the Loire. Either way, they are planning to renew their search after the baby is born. Initially they plan to spend two to three months a year in France, renting to family and friends for the rest to cover their overheads. They have even named their baby 'Sophie' so she will be just as at home in France as in England. Peter and Sharon are a couple bent on realizing their dream, even if it takes a little longer than they originally planned.

Ex-pats

Loire Valley
Robert and Susan Kirk

As the days of Margaret Thatcher went on, five-day holidays in France weren't quite enough for Robert Kirk, owner of a business manufacturing concrete, and his wife Susan. 'We loved the land, the food, the sun and the people of the Loire valley. They say where you have vines, you have smiling people and it's true. We've never found the same warmth elsewhere.' In those days, Susan used to brush up her schoolgirl French by reading French newspapers. Leafing through them one day, she saw an isolated barn advertised for £13,000 and the idea dawned that they could buy a wreck for nothing and make it habitable.

In 1989, after Robert had sold his business, they contacted a French estate agent who showed them five properties, the worst first. But the smarter they got, the less they suited Robert and Susan's taste. Returning to the first, a 350- to 500-year-old *corps de ferme*, they fell in love with it and signed the *compromis* there and then, paying their 10 per cent deposit on the £36,000 price. 'It had been used as a poultry farm and was in an appalling state, but we were persuaded by the enclosed courtyard made up of two houses and two barns. We just could see the potential.' To realize this potential, they rented a house nearby on a temporary basis, getting up 5:30 a.m. every day to go and scrape the chicken muck from the stones and sledge-hammer the worst of the

Susan Kirk and her husband, Robert, moved to the Loire over ten years ago.

rubble. After this stage, they cleaned the stones with a wire brush and repointed. 'We wanted to restore the place but not along modern lines. We wanted the stones in their former glory and where we couldn't, we plastered, papered and painted.' They had to get the property connected to mains electricity, and put in windows and doors. 'In fact, everything needed doing – no electricity, no water, floors were pulled up and refurbished, roofing corrected; no kitchen, loo, bathroom. You name it, we did it!' In 1991, eighteen months after buying it, they were finally able to move into the main house before converting the stables into a two-bedroom guesthouse for their three grown-up sons.

Visiting a *recuparateur* (salvage yard) business, Robert saw some old terracotta tiles and recognized he could make moulds and manufacture modern counterparts. The year after moving in, he tentatively started up a business, making concrete slabs

The Kirks bought a dilapidated poultry farm and painstakingly transformed it into a home for themselves.

('*pierre réconstituée*') to be used in churches and historic buildings. Over the years, word of mouth recommendations have brought them customers from all over France. So much so, that the business had to be moved from the barns to a bigger property nine kilometres away. One of the barns is ideal as a garage, while the second could be renovated into a house, but the Kirks just do not have the time any more to do it.

Both of them are now fluent in French. 'O-Level was enough as a springboard, but you must learn the language if you live here. The French are very accepting but can quite rightly be scornful if you don't make the effort.' Making friends with their neighbours came naturally as they worked on their house and they have found them generally supportive of their business. The only thing Susan sometimes misses from home is roast beef and Yorkshire pudding. 'But if a friend brings some beef out here, it never tastes the same as I remember it.' Ten years on, neither of them have any wish to return to England, having successfully built from scratch a home and business of their own.

Ex-pats

Côte d'Azur
Peter Dawson and Marilyn Seabrooke

'I was fed up with the treadmill of long hours, being chained to the desk and my computer. It was a reasonable life but I felt I was watching my life slip by.' So strong was the feeling that computer-development manager Peter Dawson and his new partner Marilyn Seabrooke, a trainee solicitor, decided to take off for the south of France to see what their money could buy. Marilyn's step-father was French and her sister had owned a holiday flat near Cannes for twenty years and so, without any long-term plans, they decided to explore within an hour or two's drive from the busy, expensive coastal strip. Having arranged to see a few properties off the Internet, they arrived in the Var, Provence at Easter, 2000, and threw their future to fortune.

Over their two-week holiday they saw a few houses that did nothing for them. Then, as they dejectedly drove up the track to a secluded, two-bedroom villa on a rainy Wednesday afternoon, days before they were due to go home, they saw it through the trees and nodded. Situated next to a vineyard on the edge of the small hamlet of Matourne and built thirty years ago in traditional Provençal style, the house

Above and below: Although the house was built around 35 years ago, it is very traditional in style and ambience. The surrounding oak and pine trees give welcome shade in the hot summer months and also shelter from the occasional Mistral wind.

immediately won them over. By the next afternoon, they had looked at it again and signed the *compromis*. 'We didn't do lots of research or even include any *clauses suspensives* but it all worked out OK,' remembers Peter. Returning to England, they gave notice to their employers, put their house on the market and secretly got married ('to avoid inheritance tax'). Four days after the wedding, a friend drove them, their belongings and their cat down to their new home.

'We hadn't a clear idea of how it would be – just that it wouldn't be that Monday to Friday treadmill. We were prepared to take things exactly as they came.' They had enough capital to last them for two or three years and just banked on something turning up. Since then, Peter

Above: The pool is surrounded by garden and floodlit at night. Below: The house is set within several acres of natural woodland next to the small hamlet of Matourne.

has done some computer consultancy and casual gardening while Marilyn teaches English in the *local maison des associations* (social club) where they both take French lessons. Peter has also discovered hidden talents in DIY and is using them to do up a small house in Flayosc and a studio in Aups that they have bought to rent out. They are establishing a B & B business at home, having already built a dam to ensure their garden would be watered during the summer and a chalet in the garden that they will stay in when the house is full.

They made friends by approaching one English-speaking couple in the hamlet. After that, it was just a question of being introduced to the others in the neighbourhood. 'There is an ex-pat club in Provence but we prefer to just cultivate our local contacts.' They keep in touch with their friends and family and will operate their rental business through their website at **www.peteandmaz.com**. They've deliberately adopted a low-income lifestyle, burning pinewood rather than switching on the electric central heating, growing their own vegetables, and are soon to have chickens and goats. 'The only real problem we've had was having over forty visitors during our first summer!' But by and large, life is tranquil although there is a lively social

calendar among the local villages with various concerts, plays and festivities. The local shops provide almost everything they need, although they did return from their last trip to England armed with 4,000 Tetley teabags and they occasionally yearn for Cheddar cheese and bacon rashers. But they have no second thoughts. 'This is the best thing we ever did. We'd advise anyone to escape the rat-race and follow their heart, doing what feels right. Time is a luxury so spend it wisely.'

Ex-pats

Tarne
Sandy and Emma Swinton

A three-and-a-half-year posting to Paris in the early '90s gave stockbroker Sandy Swinton and his wife Emma, a speech and language therapist, ample opportunity to explore other areas of France. 'As our assignment was coming to an end, successive holidays in the south-west made us think we might buy somewhere to return to. The landscape's rather Scottish, romantic, isolated and deeply unfashionable in the eyes of the French. We felt it was the part of the world for us and things were cheaper then.' A holiday with some friends near Montauban sealed their decision. During their last six months in Paris, they spent two weeks looking at fifty properties around Gaillac. 'We weren't very focussed when we started but as you see more, you soon find your level. We quickly realised that a £30,000 wreck would be too difficult to renovate from a distance, while the completely finished £150,000 houses weren't done up in a way we liked.' Their consequent aim was to find somewhere with land on which they could put their own stamp.

Below: One of the bedrooms, before and after.

They left France empty-handed but six months later, they returned for a holiday and decided to resume the search. An agent sent them details of five possible properties. On a cold, wet day, with rain coming almost horizontally up the valley, they approached a large, partially renovated farmhouse near Toulouse. 'We just thought, "If it looks like that on a bad day, it will be fantastic in July."' Originally built in 1870, the house had fallen into ruin until the current owner had bought it in the 1980s and restored one half of it to make a three-bedroom house. Within three months, the Swintons had bought it and, in 1997, they moved in with their three daughters for their first Easter holiday. The furniture they had in their Paris flat was transported down and they spent two weeks getting the place ship-shape.

The next two years were spent converting the other end of the house to contain three bedrooms, a bathroom, games room, pool changing rooms and outside kitchen. The former owner had moved locally and came on board as the *maître de projet* (project manager), helping to design the plans with the Swintons and sourcing local builders. Even now, when they are not there, they are fortunate in that he looks after the place for them. 'Things were made much easier by the fact that we all spoke fluent French. Nonetheless, there's always a long

Originally built in the late 1800's, the seven-bedroom farmhouse is set in three acres of secluded grounds with exceptional views towards the Pyrenees, which even at a distance of 200km can be seen on a clear day.

list of things to do each time we go. In 1999, we added the essential central heating, and the tennis court was finished in 2002. Everything has gone remarkably smoothly, but things do take much longer than you expect, thanks largely to the fact that people here know nothing of the sort of time pressures we're so used to in London.'

However, there have been minor inconveniences. 'We've had storms that have flooded the cellar, no electricity for days and mice in the pool. The temperature can rise to 45°C in the summer and plummet to minus 15°C in the winter, which is quite frightening and has meant burst pipes.' They are currently wrestling with a barn owl that has determinedly made the games room its home at the expense of the varnished floor. 'Anywhere else and we would cherish it.'

Overall the house has been an unqualified success for the Swinton family. 'We lead a completely different life here to the one we live in London. When we're here we get loads of fresh air, exercise, we play with our children and there is no desk with mounting bills. Nothing's done in a rush. I can't ever see us selling it.'

Ex-pats

Chamonix
Bob Camping

Owning and renting a property is not always the perfect solution to buying abroad that it sounds. Entrepreneur and founder of the Insalata chain of salad restaurants, Bob Camping found this out after appearing in *A Place in the Sun* and buying a property in Chamonix in the French Alps. Since then, a second ski season has passed, but Bob has frequently been unable to stay in his four-bedroom chalet. A rental agency successfully lets the property to groups of skiers and Bob has found himself having to stay in a nearby hotel. 'It's a question of juggling a bit to cover your investment. Sometimes I want to go at short notice but the place may be full. If the agency has it rented out, I'm getting £2,500 a week, while staying in a hotel costs about £500. So it would be mad to upset the arrangements.'

Bob Camping's traditional Alpine chalet is close to the ski resort of Chamonix.

For a substantial commission, the agency finds clients, maintains the property and turns on the heating before Bob arrives. Generally the arrangement works well, although Bob has once turned up at the chalet expecting it to be empty but finding it let without his knowledge. He remains quite sanguine about any damage that might be done by tenants. 'Nobody behaves worse than I do in the chalet. We play cricket with apples in the living room and there's a box-like coffee table signed by everyone who's stayed there and managed to get inside it.' He confesses he cracked the hot tub by leaving in the water which, of course, froze. Perhaps one of his wisest investments has been the housekeeper he found through the Internet. For £15 per person per day, she cleans the property and cooks breakfast, lunch and dinner.

Having stayed close to his estate agent, Antoine Terray of Alpine Apartments, Bob has made plenty of local friends although his French has not improved. 'They have all been terrific but I stupidly haven't learned their language, so I speak English to them.' But he has also found there are minuses to the life he longed for in Chamonix. 'The biggest drawback is that there are no women here. It's all hardcore skiers and climbers and surf dudes. If I'd known I'd have to go to Verbier for the nightlife I wouldn't have bought the place...' Otherwise he feels the restaurants are not as good as those in the more chic resorts and he is adamant about the taxi service. 'They are diabolical when it comes to getting a taxi late at night, so we've been known to fall asleep in all sorts of places (including an open-topped car) because we can't get home.'

However, on the plus side, buying the chalet has proved a sound investment. 'Property prices have gone sky high and now the French are annoyed they can't afford to buy here any more.' Another plus for Bob is the recent relaxation of the local planning laws which means his land is deemed big enough for him to build two

The Alps come into their own in the spring and summer, when the lush meadows are filled with wild flowers and there are plenty of opportunities for outdoor activities.

additional ten-bedroom chalets. 'The view won't be quite as good, but it will be worth it.' He is using the local architect who designed his current chalet and who has applied for planning permission for the project that they hope to have completed in time for the 2003 season. 'Ideally I would rent them privately through *The Sunday Times*, the Net and the ski shows. That should bring in £4–£5,000 per week. Realistically though, I won't have time, so I will either go on using the agency, or I might run it as a small ski company, or I might sell them and buy a smaller place in Verbier after all.'

How to buy your place in the sun

Checklists

Professionals you may need
- [ ] Estate agent
- [ ] Solicitor
- [ ] Accountant
- [ ] Surveyor
- [ ] Architect

How to find the right property
- [ ] Which country?
- [ ] Which region?
- [ ] Old or new property?
- [ ] Who will use the property and when?
- [ ] How many bedrooms and bathrooms?
- [ ] What kind of outside space – garden/garage/pool?
- [ ] Ideal climate?
- [ ] Accessibility of local facilities?
- [ ] Accessibility for visitors/tenants?
- [ ] Accessibility to main attractions of region (if letting property)?
- [ ] Will planning permission be readily forthcoming?

How to find properties
- [ ] Local estate agents
- [ ] Local newspapers
- [ ] Internet
- [ ] Foreign property magazines
- [ ] UK foreign property exhibitions
- [ ] UK national newspapers
- [ ] Home-finder agencies

Estate agents
- [ ] Check their qualifications.
- [ ] Be specific about the property you are looking for.
- [ ] Be specific about your budget.
- [ ] Line up a number of properties before you visit.

Before you buy
- [ ] Do not buy without seeing the property yourself.
- [ ] Get to know the region thoroughly.
- [ ] Consider renting in the area before you buy.
- [ ] Visit the property at different times of the day/week/year.
- [ ] Get to know the property market in the area.
- [ ] Talk to locals and ex-pats for advice.
- [ ] Use a surveyor.
- [ ] Be realistic about the amount of work needed.
- [ ] Ask what exactly is included in the asking price.
- [ ] Ask about local planning regulations.
- [ ] Check proximity to mains utilities if unconnected.
- [ ] Check for any rental restrictions attached to the property.
- [ ] Take as much advice as you can.
- [ ] Appoint a solicitor.

if buying off-plan
- [ ] Check plans for future development in the area.
- [ ] Consider how your property will differ from the show property.
- [ ] Find out whether there are any restrictions on owners in the community.
- [ ] Find out what the community charge includes.
- [ ] Investigate how much of the infrastructure has been put in place.

Working out your budget
- [ ] Cost of the property
- [ ] Hidden costs associated with the purchase
- [ ] Mortgage repayments and set-up costs
- [ ] Ongoing annual expenses, e.g. utilities, property taxes, rental costs, insurance
- [ ] Annual cost of upkeep

if restoring/renovating
- [ ] Professional fees
- [ ] Connection to mains utilities
- [ ] Access

if buying off-plan
- [ ] What is included in the price?
- [ ] Double-check money will be paid in stages.
- [ ] Retain a percentage until six months after completion.
- [ ] What is included in any maintenance charges?
- [ ] Will there be any extra outgoings?

Getting a mortgage
- [ ] Shop around to find which lender is offering the most favourable terms.
- [ ] Take into account the set-up fees.
- [ ] Be prepared to submit detailed accounts of your financial affairs.
- [ ] Decide whether to take out the mortgage in sterling or Euros.

- ☐ If buying a second home abroad, examine the benefits of taking out a home equity loan from your UK mortgage lender.
- ☐ Consider the pros and cons of an offshore mortgage.

Building, restoring, renovating

- ☐ Is planning permission granted for developing the site?
- ☐ How long before it expires?
- ☐ Will it be renewed?
- ☐ Are there other developments in the neighbourhood?
- ☐ Are there ground conditions that may affect the building work, e.g. slope, trees, type of earth?
- ☐ Is there access to mains connections?
- ☐ Check boundaries, rights of way, easements or covenants.
- ☐ Have old property checked over by a surveyor.
- ☐ Will restoration have to conform to any heritage or local council regulations?
- ☐ Are there local planning restrictions?
- ☐ Find an architect through personal recommendation.
- ☐ Be crystal-clear about your expectations.
- ☐ Go through plans with a fine-tooth comb.
- ☐ Appoint a project manager.
- ☐ Are there penalty clauses if work goes over schedule?
- ☐ Keep all receipts to set against rental costs or capital gains tax when the property is sold.

Leaving it all behind
for a permanent move

- ☐ Notify your bank, solicitor, accountant, insurance companies, life assurance companies, hire-purchase companies, credit card companies, rental companies, savings accounts, shopping accounts, companies with whom you have stocks and shares and the Inland Revenue.
- ☐ Inform the DSS.
- ☐ Cancel any subscriptions.
- ☐ Notify your doctor, dentist, optician and any other practitioners.
- ☐ Cancel relevant insurance policies.
- ☐ Give mains suppliers notice of your move.
- ☐ Send out change of address cards.
- ☐ Settle any outstanding debts.
- ☐ Give reasonable notice to your children's schools and any clubs they may belong to.
- ☐ Cancel milk delivery.
- ☐ Find homes for potted plants.
- ☐ Return library books.

for a temporary move

- ☐ Install/check your burglar alarm.
- ☐ Take out good insurance cover.
- ☐ Leave keys with a neighbour.
- ☐ Cancel all deliveries.
- ☐ Ensure your garden is looked after.

If renting a home

- ☐ Choose a reliable estate agent specializing in property management.
- ☐ Select a tenancy agreement that suits your needs.
- ☐ Clarify who is responsible for maintenance of the property.
- ☐ Compare rentals asked for similar properties before fixing on your own.
- ☐ Ask a solicitor to check the agreement with the letting agent.
- ☐ Include an allocation of responsibilities between the agent, the tenant and yourself.
- ☐ Include restrictions you wish to impose on tenants.
- ☐ Include the conditions for termination of the lease.
- ☐ Check gas and electricity comply with government safety regulations.
- ☐ Check the terms of your insurance policy.
- ☐ Make an inventory (photographic, if necessary).

What can I take with me?

- ☐ Sort out possessions ruthlessly.
- ☐ Make a list of things you want to take.
- ☐ Obtain three estimates from international removal companies.
- ☐ Clarify their conditions of transport.
- ☐ Insure against loss, theft and breakage.
- ☐ Make an inventory of possessions in transit.
- ☐ Give detailed directions.
- ☐ Hire a self-drive van for moving a smaller amount of possessions.

Making yourself at home

- ☐ Notify mains companies of your arrival date (or ask your estate agent to do so).
- ☐ Open a bank account.
- ☐ Register with a local dentist/doctor.
- ☐ Enrol the children in school.
- ☐ Check local requirements for pets (vaccines/tagging, etc.).
- ☐ Try to speak the language.
- ☐ Join in with your local community.
- ☐ Enjoy the local culture and new opportunites.

Estate agents

The Publishers and Freeform TV would like to thank the following companies for their help in making the programmes and this book:

Spain

Activa International (Costa Blanca, Costa Cálida)
C/José Huertas Morión 4B,
Edificio Belagua 2,
03180 Torrevieja, Spain
Tel: 00 34 965 707 685
Fax: 00 34 965 705 317
Email: info@ activainternational.com
www.activainternational.com

Atlas International (Costa Blanca)
Atlas House, Station Road
Dorking, Surrey RH4 1EB
Tel: 01306 879 899
Fax: 01306 877 441
Email: info@atlas-international.com
www.atlasinternational.com

Ballester (Costa del Garraf, Costa Dorada)
(Jose Ballester)
Calle esbater 30
0870 Sitges, Spain
Tel: 00 34 938 111 200
Fax: 00 34 938 111 202

Construccións Empuries CB (Girona)
Empuries C13
17487 Empuria Brava
Girona, Spain
Tel: 00 34 972 454 153
Fax: 00 34 972 453 589
Email: searle@grn.es
www.searle.ws

David Headland Associates (Costa de Azahár, Costa Blanca, Costa del Sol)
67 Wellingborough Road
Rushden
Northants, NN10 9YG
Tel: 01933 353 333
Email: info@headlands.co.uk
www.headlands.co.uk

Fincas la Isla (Fliprop.S:L:) (Menorca)
Sárravaleta,22
07702 Mao
Menorca, Spain
Tel: 00 44 971 365 454
Fax: 00 44 971 365 985

Email: mailto:fincas@fincaslaisla.com
www.fincaslaisla.com

Finques Proa (Costa Brava)
(Albert Jutglar)
Placa d'Espanya 4
Apartado de correos: 1096
1713010 Girona, Spain
Tel: 00 34 972 36 91 04
Fax: 00 34 972 369 104

Laybe Immobilier (San Xenxo and surrounding area)
(Javier Gomez)
Rua de Madrid 18
San Xenxo, near Pontevedra,
Galicia, Spain
Tel: 00 34 986 720 731

Look and Find (Costa Brava)
Camprodón y Arrieta, 32
(apartado de correos 1070)
17310 Lloret de Mar (Girona), Spain
Tel: 00 34 972 366 600
Fax: 00 34 972 364 040
e-mail: erwinclaasen@look-and-find.net
web: www.look-and-find.net

Marbella Homes
5 Tuthill Court
Therfield
Royston
Herts, SG8 9TT
Tel: 01763 287 372
Email: info@marbella-homes.com
www.marbella-homes.com

Quasar Homes (Galicia)
(Frank Gomez)
Apartado 55
36300 Baiona
Pontevedra, Spain
Tel: 00 34 986 385 024
Email: sgomez@anit.es
www.quasar-e.com

Remax (Sitges and surrounding areas)
Calle San Francisco 38
Sitges 08870, Spain
Tel: 00 34 610 267 189
Fax: 00 34 938 944 266
Email:philashwell@remaxlaestacion.com
www.remax.es

Rustic Bisbal (Girona)
Avenida las Boltes 32
La Bisbal 17100, Spain
Tel: 00 34 972 644 020
info@rusticbisbal.com
www.rusticbisbal.com

Rusticas del Noreste (North and Central)
C/Fray Luis de Granada, 14
37007 Salamance, Spain
Tel: 00 34 986 731 121
Email: sez_a@offcampus.net
www.rusticas.com

Sol de Andalucia
Evde. Constitución 23
E-29754 Competa
Malaga, Apain
Tel: 0131 538 3188
Tel/fax : 00 34 952 553 638
Email: soldeandalucia@spa.es
www.soldeandalucia.com

Spanish House (Sitges and Barcelona area)
By appointment only
Tel: 00 34 938 113 053
Fax: 00 34 938 113 054
Email: office@spanishhouse.com
www.spanishhouse.com

Spanish Liaisons Ltd (Costa del Sol, Malaga, Southern Spain)
Plaza Azaha 9
Coin, 29100 Malaga, Spain
Tel: 00 34 952 454 175
Email: info@spanishliasons.com
www.spanishliaisons.com

Taylor Woodrow (Majorca, Menorca, Malaga, Alicante)
Calle Aragón223,
07008 Palma de Majorca,
Majorca, Spain
Tel: 00 34 971 706 570
Fax: 00 34 971 706 565
Email: twbaleares@btitel.es

World Class Homes (Costa Brava, Costa Blanca, Costa de Sol, Costa de Orihuela, Menorca, Majorca)
22 High Street, Wheathampstead, Hertfordshire AL4 8AA
or
18 Queen Street
Mayfair
London, W1X 8JN
Tel: 01582 832001
Fax: 01582 831071
Email: info@worldclasshomes.co.uk
www.worldclasshomes.co.uk

Portugal

Algarve Homes
Largo de Rossiol
8000-721 Santa Barbara de Nexe,
Faro, Portugal
Tel : 00 351 289 99 2625
Fax: 00 351 289 99 2598/2627
Email: algarvehomes@mail.telepac.pt
www.algarvehomes.com

Alpha Property Centre (Central Algarve)
Rua Elias Garcia Nº 28
Silves 8300-155
Algarve, Portugal
Tel: 00 351 282 44 1220
Fax: 00 351 282 44 1221
email: alpha.pc@clix.pt

Donaldsons Chartered Surveyors
(Lisbon)
Rua Sao Joao da Mata 39
1200-846, Lisbon, Portugal
Tel: 00 351 213 96 3696
Fax: 00 351 213 96 3703
Email: donaldsons@netcabo.pt
www.donaldsons.co.uk

ERA (Minho)
(Carlos Simoes)
Avenida Antonio Sergio 715
4730-711 Vila Verde, Portugal
Tel: 00 351 253 32 1390
Fax: 00 351 253 22 1392
Email: vilaverde@eraportugal.com

Euroinvest (Algarve, Porto)
(Rui Ferreira)
Rua de Gontinhaes, 117
Loja A.
Vila Praia d'Ancoria, Portugal
Tel: 00 351 258 95 1319
Email: euroinvest@mail.telepac.pt

Property Search Portugal (most areas)
(Mike Carr)
Casa Andorhinas
Vale do Covo
8400-504 Prata d. Carvociro
Algarve
Portugal
Tel. 00 351 282 35 9056

Remax (most areas)
Frei Bartolomeu dos Martyres 181-183
Viana dos Castellos 4900-364
Portugal
Tel: 00 351 258 80 6150
Fax: 00 351 258 80 6159
Email: remaxviana@yahoo.com
www.remax-portugal.com

West Coast Real Estate (Lisbon, Algarve)
Centro Comercial Bugio
Loja 36
Rua Alfredo Lopes Vilaverde
2780-555 Paco de Arcos
Portugal
Tel: 00 351 214 41 8652
Fax: 00 351 214 41 9997
westcoast@talk21.com

Italy

Arciada Rete Immobiliare (Puglia)
(Felica Tamborra)
Corso Sonimo 105,
70126 Bari, Italy
Tel: 00 39 0805 586862
www.arcadia-case.it

Brian French and Associates (Tuscany,
Umbria, Le Marche, Aruzzo, Liguria)
The Neuk
Sowerby Street
West Yorkshire, HX6 3HA
Tel: 0870 730 1910
Fax: 0870 730 1911
Email: louise.talbot@brianfrench.com
www.brianfrench.com

Casa Travella (The Lakes, Liguria,
Eastern and Western, Tuscany, Rome,
Sardegna, Piemonte, Le Marche)
65 Birchwood Road
Wilmington
Kent, DA2 7HF
Tel: 01322 660988
Email: casa@travella.f9.co.uk
www.casatravella.com

Gabetti Malga (Puglia)
(Tilde Gaudio)
Via Verdi 8
74015 Martina Franca, Italy
Tel: 00 39 0804 306853
www.gabetti.it

Gabetti-Ostuni (Puglia)
(Marinella Sasso)
Tel: 00 39 0831 30611

Gruppoinvest D'Amico (Puglia)
Via Ceglie 15/17,
72014 Cisternino
Brindisi, Italy
Tel: 00 39 8044 46499
Fax: 00 39 8044 47215
Email:info@damicogruppo.it
www.damicogruppo.it

Immobiliare Bologna
(Vilma and Marco Antezzo)
Via dell'Arbiente 2B,
Ozanodell'Emiela
Bologna, Italy
Tel: 00 39 0517 98421
Email: euro@reteimmobiliaribo.it
Email: marco75@katamail.com

Piedmont Properties
Tenuta la Quiete
San Marzano,
Olivetto, Italy
Tel: 01344 624 096
Fax: 08701 641 543
Email: angelica@piedmont.co.uk
www.piedmont.co.uk

Tecnocasa (Bologna)
(Luca Vincenzi)
Via Irnesio, Bologna, Italy
Tel/Fax: 00 39 051 63 90 245
Email: BOLG1@tecnocasa.it

Tecnocasa (Ravenna)
Via Maggior 22
48100 Ravenna, Italy
Tel: 00 39 0544 21 92 01
Email: racs2@tecnocasa.it

Tuscany-on-Thames (Tuscany)
43 Webster Gardens
London, W5 5NB
Tel: 0208 579 2037/0777 551 4751
Fax: 0208 579 2037
Email: info@tuscany-on-thames.com
www.tuscany-on-thames.com

Tuscana Verde (Tuscany)
Greyhound House,
23-24 George Street,
Richmond, Surrey TW9 1HY
Tel: 07092 174660
Email: info@toscanaverde.co.uk
www.tuscanaverde.co.uk

France

Abry Immobilier (Issoire)
(Guy Roche)
33 rue Berbiziale
63500 Issoire
France
Tel: 00 33 473 55 26 26
Email: guy.roche@abry.fr
www.abry.fr

Agence Hamilton (Midi-Pyrénées, Languedoc)
30 Rue Armagnac
11000 Carcassonne, France
Tel: 00 33 468 72 48 38
Fax: 00 33 468 72 62 26
Email: info@agence-hamilton.com
www.agence-hamilton.com

L'Agence Lespinasse (Lot)
12, place de l'abbaye
46200 Souillac, France
Tel : 00 33 05 65 37 80 37
Fax : 00 33 05 65 37 80 45
Email : infos@immolot.com
www.immolot.com

L'Agence Turpault (Lot)
(Aubert Mourghen)
10 Bd. Juskiewenski
46100 Figeac, France
Tel/Fax: 00 33 565 34 63 54
Email: infos@maisons-du-quercy.com
www.maisons-du-quercy.com

Agence des Vignes (Burgundy, Saône et Loire, Côte d'Or)
20 Rue Carnot
BP 34,
21 201 Beaune, Cedex, France
Tel: 00 33 380 22 35 13
Fax: 00 33 380 22 68 58
Email: agence-des-vignes@wanadoo.fr
www.agencedesvignes.com

A.S Immo Conseils (Burgundy)
Rue Charles Rollet, La Montagne,
21200 Beaune, France
Tel: 00 33 380 24 70 20
Fax: 00 33 380 22 32 92
Email s.rerolle@proprietes-en-bourgogne.com
www.proprietes-en-bourgogne.com

Francois Wellebrouck (Loire)
3 Place de Pierre Brosse,
37130 Langeais, France
Tel: 00 33 247 45 21 22
Fax: 00 33 247 45 2/ 24
www.atoimmobilier.com

Gambetta Immobilier (Lot)
93 Bd. Gambetta
46 000 Cahors, France
Tel: 00 33 565 35 00 67
Fax: 00 33 565 53 07 08
Email:
gambettaimmobilier@wanadoo.fr
www.crdi.fr/immo

Immo Sud (Mirepoix and surroundings)
Place des couverts 09500,
Mirepoix, France
Tel: 00 33 561 68 26 49
Fax: 00 33 561 68 26 45
Email: immosud@club-internet.fr
www.immo.sud.com

Immobilier Jacques Vernudachi (most areas)
(Claudine Le Prince)
Place Savoie Villars
37350 Le Grand Pressigny
Descartes, France
Tel: 00 33 247 59 86 75
Fax: 00 33 247 91 00 98
Email: vernudachi@orpi.com
www.orpi.com/vernudachi

Impact Immobilier (South Vendée, Charente Maritime)
Fontenay le Comte
France
Tel: 00 33 251 69 71 09
Email:geoffball@wanadoo.fr

La Manche Immobilier (Normandy)
25 Rue de Villedieu
50000 Saint Lo, France
Tel: 00 33 233 05 14 07
Fax: 00 33 233 05 08 00
Email:lamanche.immobilier@wanadoo.fr

Latitudes (most areas)
Grosvenor House
1 High Street
Edgware, Middlesex HA8 7TA
Tel: 020 8951 5155
Fax: 0208951 5156
Email: sales@latitudes.co.uk
www.latitudes.co.uk

North & West France Properties Ltd
Park Lodge
Park Road
East Twickenham TW1 2PT
Tel: 0208 891 1750
Fax: 0208 891 1760
Email: sales@all-france-properties.com
www.all-france-properties.com

Patrick Desfloquet (Normandy)
Actimmo 14
35 Place de la Republique,
14100 Lisieux, France
Tel: 00 33 231 48 26 16
Fax: 00 33 231 31 26 32
Email: actomm014@wanadoo.fr
www.actimm014.com

Planchon Immobilier
20 Quai Jeanne d'Arc
37500 Chinon, France
Tel: 00 33 247 93 23 00
Fax: 00 33 247 93 35 00
Email: info@agence-planchon.com
www.agence-planchon.com

Propriétés Roussillon
29 Aversley Road
Kings Norton
Birmingham
B38 8PD
Tel: 0121 459 9058
www.proprietes-roussillon.com
Email: sales@proprietes-roussillon.com

Residences 2
55 Rue Thermale
63400 Chamalieres, France
Tel: 00 33 470 41 33 22
Fax: 00 33 470 41 33 19
Email: :residences2@wanadoo.fr
www.residences2.com

Sarl St Andre
La Cour Vauquelin (Normandy)
14130 Saint André d'Hébertot, France
Tel 00 33 231 65 43 66
Fax 00 33 231 65 48 06
Email:sarlstandre@wanadoo.fr
www.courvauquelin.com

Strategie Immobilier (Saône et Loire)
5, Rue du Puitsfeuillot
71390 Buxy, France
Tel: 00 33 385 92 05 04
Fax: 00 33 385 92 10 00
Email: strategie.immobilier@wanadoo.fr
www. Fnaim.fr/strategie

VEF (many areas)
4 Raleigh House
Admiral's Way
London E14 9SN
Tel: 020 7515 8660
Email: info@vefuk.com
www.vefuk.com

Useful Addresses

General

Department of Social Services and Overseas Benefits (DSS)
Newcastle upon Tyne
NE98 1BA
Tel: 0191 218 7777
www.dss.gov.uk

Federation of Overseas Property Developers' Agents and Consultants
95 Aldwych
London WC2B 4JF
Tel: 020 8941 5588
www.fopdac.com

The National Association of Estate Agents
21 Jury Street
Warwick
CV34 4EH
www.naea.co.uk/international/overseas

British Association of Removers (BAR)
58 Station Road
North Harrow
Middlesex, HA2 7SA
Tel: 0208 861 3331
www.bar.co.uk

John Howell & Co
Solicitors and International Lawyers
17 Maiden Lane
Covent Garden
London WC2E 7NL
Tel: 020 7420 0400
Fax: 020 7836 3626
www.legal21.org
Email: London@london21.org

France

French Government Tourist Office
178 Picadilly
London W1V 0AL

French Consulate General
21 Cromwell Road
London SW7 2EN

French Embassy
58 Knightsbridge
London SW1X 7JT

French Chamber of Commerce
21 Dartmouth Street
London SW1H 9BP
Tel: 020 7304 4040
www.ccfgb.co.uk

Fédération Nationale des Agents Immobiliers et Mandataires (FNAIM)
129 rue Faubourg St Honoré
75008 Paris
Tel: 00 33 144 20 77 00
www.fnaim.fr

Spain

Spanish Tourist Office
22/23 Manchester Square
London W1M 5AP
Tel: 020 7486 8077

Spanish Embassy
24 Belgrave Square
London SW1X 8QA
Tel: 020 7235 5555

Spanish Consulate General
20 Draycott Place
London SW3 2RZ
tel: 020 7589 8989

Spain Expat
Online resource with useful links for those living in Spain
www.expatexpert.com

Italy

Italian State Tourist Board
1 Princes Street
London W1R 8AY
Tel: 020 7408 1254

Italian Consulate General
38 Eaton Place
London SW1X 8AN
Tel: 020 7235 9371

Italian Embassy
14 Three Kings Yard,
London W1K 4EH
Tel: 020 7312 2200

The Informer-Buroservice
An excellent online magazine for ex-pats
www.informer.it

Portugal

Portuguese National Tourist Office
22/25a Sackville Street
London W1X 1DE
Tel: 0906 364 0610

Portuguese Consulate General
62 Brompton Road
London SW3 1BJ
Tel: 020 7581 8722

Portuguese Embassy
11 Belgrave Square
London SW1X 8PP
Tel: 020 7235 5331

Association of Portuguese Estate Agents (APEMI)
Rua D. Luís de Noronha,
Edifício D. Luís de Noronha
nº 4, 2º Andar
Lisboa P-1069-165
Portugal
Tel: 00 351 217 92 8770
Fax: 00 351 217 95 8815
Email: apemi@mail.telepac.pt
www.apemi.pt

A.F.P.O.P. (Association of Foreign Property Owners in Portugal)
AFPOP Head Office:
R. Infante D. Henrique, 22 2nd floor,
8500-668 Portimão
Portugal

Or write to them at.
Apartado 728,
8501-917 Portimão
Portugal
Tel: 00 351 282 45 8509
Fax: 00 351 282 45 8277
E-mail: info@afpop.com

Almancil sub-office
Tel: 00 351 289 39 8010

Further Reading

General

The Daily Telegraph Guide to Living Abroad by Michael Furnell and Phillip Jones, Kogan Page, 1986

Spain

Live and Work in Spain and Portugal by Jonathan Packer, Vacation Work, 1998

Living in Spain by Bill Blevins and David Franks, BlevinsFranks, 2000

Spain by Angus Mitchell and Tom Bell, Phoenix, 1998

Traditional Houses of Rural Spain by Bill Olds, Collins and Brown, 1995

You and the Law in Spain by David Searl, Santana Books, 2001

Portugal

Buying a Home in Portugal by David Hampshire, Survival Books, 1998

Buying a Property in Portugal, Information Book, Portuguese Chamber of Commerce

Live and Work in Spain and Portugal by Jonathan Packer, Vacation Work, 1998

Living and Working in Portugal by Sue Tyson-Ward, How To Books, 2000

Living in Portugal by Bill Blevins and David Franks, Blackstone Franks, 1995

Italy

Buying a Home in Italy by David Hampshire, Survival Books 2001

Live and Work in Italy by Victoria Pybus, Vacation Work, 1998

Living and Working in Italy by Nick Daws and David Hampshire, Survival Books, 2001

Traditional Houses of Rural Italy by Paul Duncan, Collins & Brown, 1993

France

Buying a Home in France by David Hampshire, Survival Books, 2001

Buying and Renovating Property in France by J. Kater Pollock, Flowerpoll Ltd., 2000

Buying and Restoring Old Property in France by David Everett, Robert Hale, 1999

French Law for Property Buyers edited by Kerry Schrader, French Property News Ltd., 1997

The Grown-Ups Guide to Living in France by Rosanne Knorr, Ten Speed Press, 2000

Letting French Property Successfully by Stephen Smith and Charles Parkinson, PKF Ltd.

Living in France by Bill Blevins and David Franks, Blevins Franks, 2000

Make Yourself at Home in France, Chambre de Commerce Française de Grande Bretagne, 2000

Taxation in France, 2001 by Charles Parkinson, PKF Ltd, 2001

Traditional Houses of Rural France by Bill Olds, Collins and Brown

General travel guides

The Lonely Planet Guides published by Lonely Planet Publications

The Rough Guides published by The Rough Guides

Thomas Cook Travellers' Guides published by Thomas Cook

Eyewitness Travel Guides published by AA Guides

Insight Guides published by APA Publications

Magazines

FRANCE

Everything France, call 01342 871727 for details

France, call 01451 833208 for details

French Magazine, call 01225 786800 for details

French Property News, call 0208 543 9868 for details

Focus on France, call 01323 725040 for details

SPAIN

Spain, call 0131 226 7766 for details

Spanish Homes, call 020 8469 4381 for details

ITALY

Italy, call 01305 267207 for details

GENERAL

World of Property Magazine, call 01323 725040 for details

Homes Overseas, call 020 7939 9888 for details

Property Exhibitions

Homes Overseas Exhibitions, call 020 7939 9888 for details

World of Property, call 01323 726 040 for details

Bologna show
Montagna Vende
(Bert Malca Renzi)
Tel: 00 39 0516 779570
Email: renzib@libero.it
or montagnavende@yahoo.it

Overseas Mortgages
Why use Propertyfinance4less?

- Experienced bilingual team will guide you every step of the way.
- Wide range of mortgage lenders available.
- Availability of Mortgage Payment Plan which gives you fixed monthly sterling payments.

Visit our website for more information and a personalised quote

www.propertyfinance4less.com

Tel: +44 (0) 20 7924 7314

The4LessGroup

Why pay more when you can get propertyfinance4less?